Stotts

POWER AND PRESENCE

POWER AND PRESENCE

A THEOLOGY OF RELATIONSHIPS

DON KIMBALL

1817

Harper & Row, Publishers, San Francisco

Cambridge, Hagerstown, New York, Philadelphia, Washington
London, Mexico City, São Paulo, Singapore, Sydney

Library of Congress Cataloging-in-Publication Data

Kimball, Don.
    Power and presence.

    1. Pastoral theology. 2. Theology, Practical.
I. Title.
BV404.K56   1987   253   86–45812
ISBN 0-06-254807-7

---

87   88   89   90   91   HC   10   9   8   7   6   5   4   3   2   1

In appreciation to those who have
raised me
taught me
and
loved me,

I dedicate this book to
the next person
each of us
will meet.

Contents

Foreword

Books are not written in a vacuum. This one rises out of years of work with youth and youth ministers all over North America. It also rises out of Father Don Kimball's personal experience of God's Revelation of himself, about which he writes so familiarly in these pages. But there is also evidence here of the keen intelligence and quick wit that have enabled Don to take some very profound truths and present them, not in the precise language of the professional theologian, but in the simple, straightforward and sometimes poetic language of everyday life.

Through the years Don Kimball, whom I am proud to count as a friend and former student, has discussed his experiences and insights with me and we have often wrestled over some of his approaches. Most of the time, when I have been negative in the beginning, I have come to see his viewpoint in the end. Once or twice it has even been the other way around!

This book should do a tremendous amount of good. Pope Paul VI once wrote, "What matters is to evangelize human culture and cultures . . . always taking the person as one's starting point and always coming back to the relationships of people among themselves and with God."

This book is a response to that challenge. I hope it will have the wide acclaim it justly deserves.

John R. Quinn
Archbishop of San Francisco

Preface

This is a book for all the people closest to my heart: those who try each day to love and be loved, while naming that love Jesus Christ.

You are children, youth, young adults, and adults. You are parents, singles, teens, clergy, religious, and laity, each struggling to make God's love more real in your own life as well as in the lives of the people you touch. You worry about the world's problems, while trying to survive your own.

Many of you have had little, if any, theological training. But you have had the experiences that theology talks about. I almost called this book *Practical Theology*, but I feared some people would think it trivial.

In any case, this book is for you: ministers on the front lines of contact with everyday people leading everyday lives. Maybe you wouldn't think of calling yourself a minister, but if you love, you are proclaiming the kingdom of God. If you name your unconditional love as God's, you are helping others grow spiritually. Simply put: love is ministry, whether that love is named or unnamed.

I have been blessed by working with thousands of people in ministry over the past eighteen years, and this book is a theological reflection on what I perceive to be the main issues for professional, volunteer, and even casual ministers. Most of my encounters with these people have allowed me to hear about their experiences and concerns; their successes and failures; their prayer life and their fears; their relationships with God, others, themselves, and the world around them; and, finally, their ways of "imaging" those relationships. Sooner or later, our dialogues zeroed in on two preoccupations: *effectiveness* and *survival*. How am I doing? Can I keep doing this any longer?

I believe this book can help sort out the facts and feelings as well as the images and the choices it takes to remain a Christian minister in the modern world.

May this book be a continuing tool of friendship between you and me, between you and others, and between God and all of us.

It's good being on earth with you!

Author's Note on Language
A Theology in Search of a Pronoun

In writing this book, I've found it hard to balance the traditional images of God with the exciting and disturbing images currently under discussion within the church. As you may know, the gender of God (if God has a gender) is the subject of much debate in speculative theology.

When it comes to pronouns referring to ordinary people like you and me, I have chosen to use inclusive language when appropriate. The pronouns for God are a much more complex issue. I devoutly believe that neither God nor the church has called me to be the one to resolve this debate at this time. But in order to get this book to you before the next century, I have had to resolve in my own mind what to do with the personal pronouns referring to God. Hybrids (*he/she*) don't work, and alternating pronouns (*he* one time; and *she* the next) makes it look to me as though God has an identity crisis.

After looking at various attempts at inclusive language, I concluded that, while I admire the attempt to balance the male and female images of God, the current formulas are still unsatisfactory.

So what did I do about personal pronouns referring to God? Nothing.

Since neither the church nor anyone else has an adequate sexually inclusive theological pronoun in standard use, I am leaving all the theological pronouns male, because male pronouns have been the standard. When a more accurate pronoun for God becomes widely accepted, I promise to revise the book accordingly.

In reaching this decision, I must say that I did some enjoyable theological reflecting, which you may find interesting. Although I suspect that the transcendent aspect of God as pure spirit has no gender at all, we still need to "image" the immanent aspect of God made visible in our midst. What does this mean for us?

In choosing to be visible to us, God chose to become human. And in choosing to become human, this genderless God had to select a gender: male or female. In choosing the male gender, God gave us the historical Jesus Christ, who reveals God becoming human. That's the central issue, not gender. God is simply working within our limitations to communicate an unlimited love.

Other than selecting either a male or female gender for this role, what other choices did God have? It was out of the question that God become human in either a genderless or an androgynous body. From Pharisees to disciples, people had enough trouble handling the message of Jesus. Imagine the chaos if Jesus had walked around in a male-female body! Or a genderless body! So a choice was made and the historical Jesus was male. But after the Resurrection and the Ascension, this same Jesus uses all of our bodies, becoming present in everyone, revealing God's power and presence in males and females alike.

So can we say that although the historical Jesus *was* male, the resurrected Jesus, living in the body of Christ, *is*, in a certain way, both male and female? Why not?

My theologian's mind soars at the possibilities. But my survivor's instinct warns me to duck my ministerial head as the church enters into a deeper and hotter discussion of this issue. Theological facts and images are at stake here. How will we continue perceiving ourselves, God, Jesus, church, and ministry?

And pronouns?

PART ONE:
RELATIONAL THEOLOGY

1. The World Has Changed

Every generation has its strengths and weaknesses, and the church in each generation must find a way to work with these strengths and weaknesses to continue its mission of proclaiming the good news in every culture, language, art form, and human condition. Down through the centuries the church has succeeded best when the believers of an era were able to worship the Lord "with every voice and tongue" (Rev. 14:6) and find ways to proclaim their experience of God "to all nations" (Matt. 28:19).

On the one hand, history judges the church most sharply when believers—apparently well intentioned—tried to convert the way of life of the listener to fit the way of life of the proclaimer. Catholic countries in the First World often discovered too late that they were preaching an encultured form of the gospel, rather than a gospel whose images could be adapted to the culture of the newly evangelized.

On the other hand, the church can be seen as accomplishing its mission at Pentecost, when each member of the audience heard the good news in his or her own tongue. The Renaissance is another example of how the artistic expressions of the day spoke to the hearts of the beholders. Many old liturgical songs, considered bedrock items in worship today, originated in the Renaissance as adaptions of bar songs. Again, during the Agricultural Revolution the church clarified its message and presented that message in terms that people of the time could understand. Jesus himself uses many agricultural terms to reveal the kingdom. Yet again, in the Industrial Revolution the church found itself challenged to speak in the language of workers, employers, factories, transportation, and mechanized civilization.

Today it appears that two parallel revolutions will continue to change significantly the way we live. The Communications

Revolution has made it easier to send and receive information, and the media have bombarded us with expanded options in programming, live coverage, and advertising.

The Computer Revolution has also given us access to information, although it does not bombard us with it. Currently the greatest impact on our lives is in education and in the reorganization of our economy, especially in the area of financial transactions.

So the Communications Revolution puts us in touch with more people, more ways of life and more products than ever before, and the Computer Revolution offers us access to more information in one hour than most people had available in a lifetime 100 years ago, and we can buy products more efficiently. We can also see in the merging of these technologies a more efficient way of destroying our enemies—and ourselves and our world as we know it.

We are in a new age which, like any other age, has its own strengths and weaknesses, as well as drastic new consequences. As a church, we still have our historic mission of proclaiming the good news, which includes the challenge to present our experience of the Lord in the language of the day. We still have the Lord, his power, and his presence, and we need to ask the people we meet certain questions. Are they happy, satisfied, at peace? Do they know they are loved totally, permanently, today, now? Do they love anyone else, or even know how to love? And do they know that the unconditional love in their experience is God? If not, we have a message.

All of these questions are relational questions. Relationships: you and I; we and they; God and us. Our new tehnologies can either help us love and be loved, or they can help destroy us. Ultimately the question is, Will we be communicating person to person or terminal to terminal? Will we be loving or hating? Will we be in conversations with God or groping at a constantly accelerating pace for material, tangible satisfaction? Will we be alive, living, and loving? Or will we be living in the past, or the future, but not living now, not loving now? All relational questions; all theological questions; all with answers, and all the answers are persons: God, others, and myself.

Because the world is changing, the church must change with it. We won't change any essentials, but we will need to change our technique, our approach, our style of presentation. Models of ministry considered vital in the past may need to be updated, not because they were bad in their day, but because they are not as effective in responding to what people need today.

As a way of bringing this into focus, let's look at the way the world has changed our appreciation of all our structured relationships, the sociological and religious experience we call community.

In the 1930s a person could expect to grow up in at least four major communities: a family, a church, a school, and a civic body (town or neighborhood). Education was a process of teaching an individual how to live in these communities. Religious education continued the process by defining and clarifying the Christian way of life in each of these communities, with a particular emphasis on behavior. Reliable and systematized behavior in a community is a role: father, mother, child, Christian, priest, religious, layperson, teacher, citizen, and so on. Education was considered successful when students learned how to live correctly within a given community. This system worked as long as the communities stayed intact and the roles and behavioral codes of these communities remained reliable. It was unthinkable that the four communities would change significantly. But in the past fifty to sixty years, the unthinkable has happened.

Today these four communities have changed significantly, and in many cases have deteriorated to the point that the roles and behavioral codes previously held sacred no longer match the experience of the student. When we taught a religion class about God as Father, we used to assume that any student could relate positively to the image of father; we didn't have to teach that too! That was an accepted role in the family comunity. But today, for more than half the students in a classroom, that word *father* does not connote a positive experience; it may not in fact, suggest any experience at all! The teacher may say "God is our Father," or the class may pray the "Our Father," and a large number of students will think: "Father? Oh, yeah. Father. He's the one who left home three years ago." Or, "He's the one who was stumbling around drunk last night, and beat me. Father? God is Father? Who needs another father like that?"

When dealing with a young person in any classroom or program today, we can no longer assume that his or her communities are intact. Over the past half-century, what has happened to our family, church, school, and civic communities? In what other age in history have we had to define individually rather than categorically what we mean when we say father, mother, child, Christian, priest, religious, layperson, teacher, citizen, and so on?

When the roles shift, society shifts. If society is the sum of its communities, and if communities operate on a reliable understanding of roles, and if roles are described and taught through behavioral codes, duties and even stereotypes, then several things should be obvious to anyone today: the definition of anything has become hazardous; roles have been scrambled; and the existence of communities can no longer be presumed. When the communities and the roles change, the very mission of teaching, maybe our whole approach to young people, must be reexamined.

In reviewing my own development as a young person in the church, I remember that I perceived the church as a system of beliefs and practices that could lead me to a deeper life with God, usually as a reward in the next life. I somehow came to understand that, in this life, the deeper life with God ordinarily came only with entry into the priesthood, religious life, or, on occasion for the layperson, with regular attendance at daily mass.

I understood faith to be the combination of knowing the list of beliefs and then practicing the behavior of a Catholic Christian. I also understood that there was something seriously wrong with other Christian and non-Christian religions, especially with *their* lists and practices.

Lists and practices: knowing and doing. And if I didn't know, do it anyway! And don't ask too many questions. Just learn the questions and the answers supplied to me. This was what God and the church wanted.

One strong focus of this system was on the digest of beliefs:

summaries of belief statements that were organized for easier learning into lists. The collections of these lists and practices became catechisms. I also remember that numbers helped us to memorize. One list went like this:

One: God
Two: Natures in Jesus Christ: God and man
Three: Persons in God
Four: Gospels
Five: The Pentateuch: the first five books of the Bible
Six: Laws of the church in the United States; holy days of obligation
Seven: Sacraments
Eight: Beatitudes
Nine: First Fridays; novenas (nine consecutive days of prayer)
Ten: Commandments
Eleven: The apostles without Judas
Twelve: The apostolic community, successor to the twelve tribes

The system also placed an emphasis on the history of the church, especially the lives of its saints. We were to study their behavior, imitate their lives, and try to foster sanctity by doing what they did—more practices.

Because I understood faith as beliefs and practices, it made sense that the task of religious education was to pass on the faith. This task was done jointly by parents and teachers, but mostly by teachers, because they were better trained.

The task of religious education meant teaching the beliefs and practices until the student internalized them in the form of memorized lists and formulas, which led to the development of spiritual habits. Developing good habits was important. This whole system of religious education was reinforced by consistent teamwork involving parents, teachers, and clergy. On paper, it was a good system, the result of centuries of experience of many God-centered people. And in the secular world, many corporations followed a similar method.

Roles and rules were crucial to this system. To have good order in the community, both were vital. So roles were clearly defined, and rules were strictly enforced for the good of the community. The student was educated in the role options available and encouraged to strive for the higher roles. In the church setting, these higher roles clearly yielded higher rewards, resulting in closeness with God in this life and in the next. Is it any wonder that people worked diligently on their practices, right down to a simple detail such as folding their hands properly during worship and private prayer?

With beliefs and practices concretized so clearly, it should be easy to see how studying lists and imitating the saints while practicing the faith eventually became norms, which were then spelled out as rules.

But rules have at least two major weaknesses:

• People faithfully carrying out the rules may never know why these rules are so important, and they may not even be invited to discover why. "Don't question!" they are told.
• Rules are behavioral codes set up on the assumption that the communities anchoring these roles will not change significantly.

Rules are great for providing order in the community, but when their meaning is sacrificed, we are left vulnerable to the same critique Jesus leveled at the Pharisees: "These people honor me with their lips, but their heart is far from me" (Mark 7:6, quoting Isa. 29:13).

The meaning of the good news is love: God's love for us and the invitation for us to accept that love already within us, but not forced upon us. Love assumes relationships in which that love is shared. And most of our relationships are found somewhere within our communities.

So when our communities deteriorate, or our understanding of roles within these communities is scrambled (leaving us to practice religious behavior without meaning and without loving relationships with God, others, or even ourselves), then the application of rules alone does not make any sense.

When that happens, we have two choices. Either we panic at the thought of our deteriorating communities and continue to operate an educational system dependent on these communities, or we start rebuilding these communities first. And as we do that, we will find ourselves clarifying our current experiences of God, others, and ourselves, and reconnecting these ongoing events of love to the church's history of belief and traditions of worship. We will find that our tradition is quite flexible in the light of ongoing experiences of God, a faith in the God who deals with us today. This same God will help us rebuild our communities and clarify our beliefs, while we critically review our rules and practices.

No one wants to throw out community, beliefs, practices, or even some rules. But in a world that is changing very fast, there will be many points of view about which models best support and present our religious experiences. For example, for some in the church, building community has never been a part of their faith experience. Communities have just been there, so living in them has been the focus. For them, private spirituality has been the central issue, a personal prayer life that is no one else's business. People of this persuasion might view as trivial the efforts of today's community builders who are getting together to know each other better and to share their faith.

I remember approaching a pastor of a parish about building a youth group in the parish, showing him that such a group would let the young people learn to relate more easily to each other while at the same time allowing them to share their experiences of God with each other at their meetings. His response was classic: "They don't need a youth group. They should be going to mass on Sunday. That's enough. And if they don't do that, they go to hell. It's as simple as that."

People in the ministry who see the need to rebuild families, worshiping communities, schools, and civic groups will come into sharp conflict with those in both secular and religious education who are asking, "Where's the content? Where are the formulas? What happened to sin? How do we discipline those who operate outside accepted behavioral codes?"

So as the world changes, conservatives will want to get back to previously defined roles, while more liberal people will want to experiment with new roles. Actually, it looks as though neither a reinstatement of the old roles, nor a wholesale replacement of these roles will be the answer. The answer, instead, will be somewhere within the ongoing world of relationships. Who loves you? Do you love anyone else? These questions will always be at the center of religious and secular meaning. In religious education, of course, building relationships cannot be our only activity before we get down to it and really teach religion. But if the contents of all teachings were to be summarized, we would find that we should, in the words of Jesus, "Love one another as I have loved you" (John 15:12).

To love, you have to relate to someone. Can you imagine trying to love someone *outside* of a relationship? Try it! So loving and relating aren't just the beginning of a religious growth; loving is the goal of the process as well. Jesus again: "Love the the Lord your God . . . and your neighbor as yourself" (Mark 12:30,31). He was summarizing the whole law into a set of loving relationships with God, others, and self. Content can only help us love better. It is a tool, just as lists, practices, and rules are only tools, even though important ones.

We need to reconnect people to one another, and, as we will see shortly, this is where we will find God doing his best work. In many church services, we remain strangers while worshiping in ceremonies that call us to love one another. If we are going to carry out this command of Christ, we are going to have to rebuild our relationships into daily events that reveal God, others, and ourselves. From that experience will come the renewal of the whole church in a changing world. We will find ourselves keeping what is essential and updating everything else. One thing that cannot change is Jesus Christ calling us to love and be loved, showing us his Father, guided by the Holy Spirit.

Organizations and programs and classes can only gather people. Who will love those who are gathered? Who will allow themselves to be loved? To answer these real-life questions we will have to look at our relationships and rebuild our communities person to person, discovering the Lord in our midst as we go. In the process, we will find ourselves perfectly faithful to the best of church tradition, while living in this real world that is desperate to hear some good news. As a friend of mine muttered about the church: "We need to get into the twentieth century before we get out of it."

This changing world, like our church programs, can only

gather people. Programs will never love you; roles will never love you. Only the Lord can be the love we all need. And he is here, among us, now.

This fact has enormous implications for teaching, parenting, and leading, in our secular society as well as in the church.

2. The Church Is Changing

Because the proclamation of the good news of God's love for all of us is central to the church's mission, the people who hear this message must be able to recognize its value to each of them personally. Telling someone about love can be a shallow exercise if the proclaimer of the message doesn't love the person being addressed. And the most effective way we can let people know the're loved by God is to show them we love them, or that God is loving them through us. Although books, flyers, banners, television, radio, and other tools can deliver the message, the most effective means of announcing God's love is to love. And this will happen somewhere within a relationship.

I remember taking a summer school class at the University of San Francisco from Fr. Bernard Häring. In that class he made a comment that both startled me and refocused my thinking about theology. He said, "All theology can be experienced somewhere in a relationship." The more I thought about that statement, the more I realized that he was profoundly on target and that my life at that point was profoundly off target.

I had grown to love studying theology. For two years prior to this class, I had been reading up to four theology books a week, fascinated with what the Vatican II theologians were writing. But all of this reading didn't come together until I heard Fr. Häring's remark. The good news was that I had experienced a moment of revelation, when everything came together into sharp focus. The bad news was that I was sadly out of position as a relational person. If all theology could be lived in relationships, I wasn't living very fully. I would need to do some changing.

That summer I began reviewing the ways I dealt with people and making some choices to learn how to be a caring person and to be more sensitive to the people who were trying to care about me. The seminary where I studied theology helped at times. I developed friendships there that still enrich my life. But some of the training seemed to try to steer me away from relationships. I vividly remember hearing a priest at one of our spiritual conferences warning us about relationships. He saw relationships as the area where temptations would occur. If you didn't actually sin in a relationship, then at least you would be entering the territory called the near occasion of sin. The message was clear: we were not only to avoid sin, but we were to avoid the near occasion of it. And relationships were the danger zone. We were not to have any "particular friendships"— nicknamed P.F.s—which meant we weren't to have any close friends or be seen with the same person a lot.

I sat in my seat as he waxed: "Now, men, God is giving you this special gift of the priesthood for the service of others, and you must do everything in your power to protect this gift. It becomes very easy to fall when you get involved too closely with other people. Keep yourself close, instead, to Christ; stay apart from the world." As you will see a little later in the book, the Incarnation makes that last item tricky!

He went on: "Now, men, you have to be especially careful in your relationships with women, because you all know what can happen when you get involved with women" (spoken with a pious snarl). I looked over at my buddy across the aisle and winked. Of course we understood what happened with women!

Still more: "And, men, you also have to be careful in your relationships with other men, because you know what can happen when you get involved with other men." Again I looked at my buddy. We'd heard what could happen.

Suddenly I sat bolt upright in my seat, horrified at the implications of what I had just heard and gasped in a whisper to my buddy, "What's left?"

It was clear then that our spirituality was centered on praying to a God who lived in a chapel, to a Lord made tangible in sacraments, but not to the God who lived in the people we were to serve, the Jesus Christ I have since come to know in the world, in my relationships, in me. Of course you sin with people. But people are also where you meet God.

Relationship building, sometimes called community building, has become the key survival skill for our society and especially for the church. I'm not talking about just organization rebuilding or urban redevelopment. Community building depends on people sharing with other people their needs and gifts, their hopes and dreams, their stuggles and victories: in essence, being part of one another's lives. Organizational details can assist, but not replace, these central personal events.

I hear a lot of people say, "I'll go back to that parish (or group) when they change the way they do things." What this means is that I'll get involved when they reorganize. But both history and spiritual wisdom have shown that a change of organization will not cause a change of heart. Personal renewal can bring about organizational renewal: that is, changed people will rebuild structures to facilitate their continued growth. I saw this sentiment on a banner in a church: If You Want Your Message To Change the World, Let It Change You First."

God's love will change you, and you'll notice that change in your interaction with others. As you discover this love, you'll share it with others. You can't give what you don't have. You can't love others unconditionally unless you are in touch with God's unconditional love for you. But when you are in touch, you'll not only improve your existing relationships, you'll be going out to build some more and help others do the same thing.

Community building, then, is primarily relationship building on three different levels: the one to one, the small group, and the large group. All of these levels involve personal relationships, some with individuals and some with groups. A full relational life means that a person can interact effectively and lovingly on all three levels. To be honest, though, I think we probably enjoy one level more than we do the others. But that shouldn't make us avoid the other two levels of interaction. For example, I've always felt most comfortable in front of a large group. In small groups, I feel fairly comfortable with the give and take, but in my one to one relationships, I have had to grow the most. I still don't think I'm very good on that level, but I'm getting better. I've noticed, though, that the more relaxed I am in one to one relationships, the better I feel in groups, so it all seems to interconnect.

In spiritual and religious growth, a person should be able to

find and share love with God, other, and self on all three relational levels. Again, one level will probably be easier than the
other two. But isn't it just like God to challenge you to grow in
areas in which you aren't yet comfortable?

What this means is that our relationship with God has a private dimension and a public dimension. "What you hear in the
dark, speak in the light" (Matt. 10:27). What Jesus heard in private prayer with his Father, he brought into his ministry. Will
it be any less for us? Of course our private prayer will need to
go public at liturgy. Of course our own personal metanoia
(change of heart) will be expressed in our outreach to others.

If we're going to rebuild our commmunities, we will do it by
rebuilding our relationships with God, each other, and even
ourselves. Sometimes this will generate new roles and rules,
new practices, and even some clearer belief statements. Other
times, we may find ourselves choosing the more traditional
roles, rules, practices, and belief statements, but living them in
a more contemporary way. Remember: activity cannot cause
faith, but faith relationships will cause activity.

Rebuilding our parish communities is a call to relationships.
Do we care about the people with whom we are gathering?
Will we let them care about us? In my first parish assignment,
our whole staff cooperated in a project that involved inviting
six couples to the rectory on Sunday nights for a dinner cooked
and served by six couples invited the previous week. In all,
twelve couples and the parish staff ate together each Sunday
night. Within a few weeks we could tell the difference this one
event was making throughout the parish.

Rebuilding our civic communities is a call to relationships.
One parish sadly closed its school because of financial difficulties, but when the students were absorbed into the public
school system, the parents as well as other adults from the parish became active in that system, all the way from becoming
playground volunteers to being elected to the board of education. The whole civic community benefited, and there was a
noticeable thaw in relations between Catholics and non-
Catholics.

Our search for happiness calls us to relationships. Who
wants to be lonely? The church preaches a message of love. I've

personally heard (and, I hope, delivered) many homilies encouraging people to get out there and love everybody. But who in the church shows people how to love, how to forgive, how to deal with loneliness, how to allow ourselves to be loved? The everyday person's search for happiness is actually a search for love.

The gospel calls us to relationships. Jesus is constantly with his Father, or with his disciples, or with the sick, the lonely, the hurting. He knows his listeners and uses the language and tools they understand. On more than ten occasions in the gospel, he shows the priority of love, even over the letter of the law. "The Sabbath was made for man, not man for the Sabbath" (Mark 2:27). For Jesus, the good news is that the kingdom is at hand, right here.

Spirituality calls us to relationships. When you're happy, it's because your spirit is happy. And your spirit is fed by love, by the conversations with God, who will always tell you at least two things during the talks you have: "I love you and always will" and "Will you pass on what I give you?" In genuine prayer we will see how much God enjoys us, but we will come to see his concern for others who don't know how loved they are.

Personal renewal calls us to relationships. When your heart returns to the Lord, when you go through each one of many ongoing conversions, you will begin to see the world with the eyes of God and love the world with the heart of God. You will love the poor without judging them, you will forgive those who hurt you without punishing them, and you will even forgive yourself easily when you forget to do the first two. The peace within you will grow and will be a resource for others who cannot find that peace within themselves yet.

Organizational renewal is also a call to relationships. If we aren't working together, then we are probably working against each other. In another parish where I worked, the pastor and I identified ten different subgroups within the parish framework. But none of these groups seemed to mix well with the other groups; each group spoke in its own code, a language not shared by the others. The Marriage Encounter group talked about weekends, couples, 10-10s, and 90-90s, and the charismatic group quoted scripture verses, sometimes not even the whole verse—just references. I saw one man walk over and put his arm around another man, obviously in love and admiration, but what came out of his mouth was "Philippians 1:4." That was it! Because no one seemed to speak a common language we invited the key leaders of each group to a series of special meetings, and everyone came who was invited, a miracle in itself! Within this group of a hundred people, we came to a common experience of God in our midst, a deep appreciation of each other, and a new excitement about our parish. Each group still had its own language code, but when we all came together, we spoke a new common language, created from our common experience. Without sacrificing anyone's uniqueness, we saw people bring that uniqueness as a gift to help the parish grow into a multidimensional community.

Liturgy calls us to celebrate and accelerate our relationships. The Greek word for liturgy means "work of the people." Liturgy was never meant to be the work of only one person, even if that person is God! It implies something we do together. The ritual can only make visible our relationships. If these relationships are growing and vital, then the liturgy will express that. If our relationships are dull and uninteresting, then the liturgy will probably be the same. A boring liturgy requires boring people.

Salvation calls for us to be loved by God in a personal relationship. When we peel all the jargon away to reveal the essentials, we see that salvation means allowing ourselves to be loved by God; this "saves" us from loneliness, both now and in the next life. Strangely enough, many people, even in the mainline churches, don't know that a personal relationship with God is possible in this life. Most of these people see the church as just a big company. God is the boss they work for; they are "just" employees, doing the job (being good in this life) that "the man upstairs" has ordered, hoping all the time to cash in on the company's benefits (heaven) when they retire (die). They pray to God and never expect a personal answer, but hope he will use his power to straighten out things in the company and in the world outside. Some relationship between the person and God *does* exist, even in this style of Christianity, and of course, God knows what's in these people's hearts. But so much more is available.

Ministry calls us to share with others the love we have accepted from God. "If you love me, feed my sheep" (John 21:17). "Don't put the light under the basket; let it shine" (Matt. 5:15). One New Year's Day I noticed that the readings told us that we had inherited the whole kingdom (Luke 12:32). So, instead of pitching the same old New Year's Resolutions theme in the homily, I saw a way to dramatize that the one thing we really needed to do with this inherited kingdom of spiritual riches was to spend the riches; otherwise, what fun were they?

So during the homily I said just that: spend, spend, spend! And to make this spiritual point tangible, I signaled the ushers to come forward. Down the aisle they came with baskets full of spiritual money I had printed up in packets of $100. (Isn't that the way an inheritance ought to be passed out?) You should have seen the expressions on the people's faces! It was the first time they had ever received anything from a collection basket! The place went wild!

I went on to tell the parishioners that this was spiritual money, from a spiritual kingdom. It wouldn't buy cars or stereos, but it could be spent on reconciliations, on prayer, on getting rid of loneliness or anger, on caring for each other, and so on. And they could spend this money as fast as they could, because the supply would never run out. To further illustrate that they could never exhaust the riches of this kingdom, the next Sunday we gave everyone in the parish a spiritual credit card, told them to go on a spiritual spending spree, and that they would never get a bill. Ministry is taking what you have been given and spending it on others.

The sacred scriptures are the written account of relationships. They came to us inspired by God and were passed on to us through a community of relationships called the church. So the scriptures are stories of real relationships that implore us to see what happens to people who will let God love them and lead them. We also see what happens to people who will not allow themselves to be loved. Whether or not the facts of the story are historical, the main point or truth of the story is the message God wants us to know. Some scriptural stories are historical and factually accurate; some are historical but include minor inaccuracies; some stories—the parables—were made up.

If Jesus made up stories in order to teach a truth (about the sower or the Good Samaritan, and so on) what's more important, the facts of the story or the truth of the story? It pains me to see religious people quarrel over data and miss the truth. The Pharisees and the Scribes did a lot of that, and of all the people in the gospels they seemed to anger Jesus the most.

Although the scriptures are the written accounts of the relationships between God and his people, this Written Tradition ended around 100 A.D. We are still guided by the revelation in and between the lines of the verses, but the scriptures don't constitute all there is to revelation. What the Written Tradition said, our Oral Tradition continues to say: the same God, the same Jesus in the Gospels, the Acts of the Apostles, and the rest of the Christian scriptures is still within us. We now continue to tell more stories of the same Jesus as *our* stories, records of the experiences we are now having. Our Written Tradition tells us what did happen and can happen between God and his people. Our Oral Tradition lets us tell what did happen and what is *still* happening.

When the Christian community gathers, we need to hear both the written word and the spoken word, the stories that promise and stories of the promises come true today!

Silence can be a sign of prayer. But it can also be a sign of death. In church, we have been reading the scriptural stories regularly. But when it comes to sharing our *own* spiritual journeys, we have been much too silent. In this case, silence is not always golden. We need more significant speaking in our gatherings.

Jesus, the word of God, is the proclamation, even as he speaks it. And he invites us to live in our relationships what we proclaim to others. In Jesus, the word is the expression of his whole personality, not just a sound coming from the mouth. Jesus doesn't *say* the word of God; he *is* that word. And the word is love. There it is again: relationships. Even creation itself is interdependent; all parts of God's work are made to work together. "And it was good" (Gen. 1:31).

Spiritual growth is a journey through relationships. We may remain in some relationships longer than others, but all are opportunities to love and be loved. All are events that can reveal God.

Just as some relationships develop without much effort on our part (with our parents, brothers and sisters, relatives, and so on), the love offered by God through our relationships is never forced. Instead, it is offered by invitation. Like a real friend, God wants to love you, wants you to be happy, but never takes away your freedom to accept his love when you're ready.

Once it *is* accepted, however, this love is facilitated by interaction. In other words, love grows when it's shared with others. Most people don't really know all of the great things love can do until they're in a relationship that allows them to see its depth and versatility.

Somewhere in this growth cycle love will be made tangible, touchable, concrete. The spiritual events of loving will need to be made physical, celebrated in word, gesture, or music. Just as faith leads to action, so will love. And this action may strengthen and accelerate the existing relationship, and it may reveal this love to others. In one form or another, love will seek expression in forms our physical senses can recognize.

This is the cycle: God's love is offered by invitation, facilitated by interaction, and celebrated in word, gesture, and music. Through celebration, the love is deepened in the celebrants, but the same words, gestures, and music may also carry new invitations to love to desperate ears and hearts, beginning a new cycle.

3. A Shift in Emphasis

In my kindergarten year at St. Rose School in Santa Rosa, California, our class was graduating in a ceremony in the school auditorium. Just to let you know the kind of kid I was, the teacher thought it clever to have me dressed as a priest—portraying the local pastor, no less—and give out the diplomas to the rest of the class. During a short speech to the audience during the pageant, I fussed with my cassock, lost my white collar, and waved to and "dialogued" with everyone in the audience I knew—including the real pastor. I don't think much of my rehearsed speech was ever delivered. So much for content.

Anyway, it rocked the audience of maybe 200 people, and it became one of the memorable moments in what was then a small town. Since then, I'm sure I've met at least 3000 people who were there and have retold the story as witnesses.

Over the remaining twenty years of Catholic education, I was exposed to a lot of content, the basic information all Catholics should know. And I know I've learned most of it. But the best memories I have of my teachers are not of what they taught me, but of the warmth they showed me. Sure, they shook their heads as they beheld the chaos my undisciplined mind created, turning to shambles an otherwise orderly and pious environment. Sure, I spent more time in the office than I did in the classroom. But they liked me for some reason, and I hold those as my best memories of my years in Catholic schools. Maybe that is the main message that should have stayed with me: that I was loved, even when I wasn't well behaved. As a little kid on stage before an audience, interacting was more important than covering the material of the speech. Since then, I saw the arrival of the dialogue mass, where the people in the pews were actually invited to talk in church, if only to recite the prayers with the priest. But we were praying the mass, not just praying at mass. A shift.

Then came mass in the vernacular. Another shift. We were praying the mass in a language we understood! Some people deplored the loss of mystery in the liturgy, but I always wanted to know why we were supposed to do what we were doing. My curious mind tends to rebel in the face of mystery, as my past theology professors would attest.

Another shift toward being more relational came with the reactivation of the sign of peace. Now at liturgy you had to touch someone, breaking the invisible shield between worshipers and reaffirming the Lord's presence in the pew as well as at the altar. One of my great moments in church history occurred while I was serving in my first assignment. Another priest in our house was celebrating Sunday mass a few weeks after the sign of peace had been reactivated, and upon wishing the whole worshiping community the peace of Christ, he started down the aisle, greeting the people at the end of each pew with the handshake. As he approached one pew, he encountered an elderly woman and offered his hand. She responded by crossing her arms and hissing, "I don't do that!" He said without pause, "Madam, if you won't shake my hand, I am going to kiss you." Maybe she was acting on the principle of the lesser of two evils, but in any case, her hand flew out, and her lips were spared.

It should be obvious that we are still experiencing a shift toward becoming more relational. Some welcome it with relief; others seem stressed over this development, viewing it as decidedly alien to the spirit of prayer and the task of learning.

Regardless of preference, this shift features a strong emphasis on the whole person, with ministry programs no longer subdivided into spiritual, intellectual, recreational, and devotional components. Because a church member might attend only one program, the meeting had better address all four areas of the individual's growth. In other words, offer an integrated approach.

This shift toward making relationships the integrating event balances a past emphasis in the opposite direction. In educational programs the information transfer process had become the sole focus, with achievement measured by tests and grades. In athletic programs the emphasis had often swung too far toward winning, with achievements measured by the final score of the game. Unfortunately, if achievement is measured only by grades or game scores, only a few can win; everyone else loses, often at a terrible cost to self-image and the quality of relationships.

In the church's shift away from education that features only the transfer of information, we are reaffirming that salvation is found not simply in accumulating knowledge. The Gnostics were condemned for this. Of course, there's nothing wrong with knowledge, but it should reveal God's invitation to accept his love, which comes through the people around us.

There's a big distinction between knowing something and knowing someone. A lot of people know about God and can recite perfectly all the information taught in religion classes. But they don't know him. There are many atheists in the world who once boasted A's in religion. Who wants to spend years studying about a God you'll never meet? Religious education will only be a complete process when teachers can reveal that a genuine relationship with God is possible in this life. And teachers will best reveal that relationship by talking about their own relationship with God and showing how that relationship has affected their contact with other people.

The distinction between knowing about God and knowing God personally may be easy to articulate, but helping people shift toward being more relational is not going to be easy. In this model of ministry, you need actual relationships before you can talk about them. And when you've been trained all your life to keep your relationship with God private, it's going to take an enormous amount of energy to encourage these same people to share their faith experiences. If you want to see on the same face a mixture of terror and confusion, just ask the average mainline Christian churchgoer to talk about his or her experience of God! You'll probably be told it's none of your business.

We can hope that as the church continues to become more relational, God's invitation to us to be loved will be extended by us, personally, to a world starving for this good news. Anyone responding to this offer will find that this unconditional love is already given by God. Accepting it requires a choice. Then passing it on becomes another choice. The first choice, accepting God's love, is salvation; the second choice, sharing that love, is ministry.

Religious information alone should not be the goal; it is a means, a tool, to help people attain their relational goal: life with God. And a noncompetitive approach to measuring our experience of God will ultimately help the people we serve as individuals, especially those who are having a difficult time growing spiritually.

Jesus' parable of the sower (Mark 4:3-8) uses an agricultural image to tell a great story of spiritual growth. Depending on whether you operate with the information transfer view or the relational view of education, however, you might interpret this parable differently. For those who are really sold on information transfer as the primary focus in education, the seed in this parable is the information, cast by the educator upon four different kinds of ground: the pathway, which has become hard from being walked on constantly; the rocky ground, which contains so many hard places that growth of the knowledge is impossible; the weeds, which are the bad influences that compete with what the individual is taught, eventually choking off any growth; and finally, the good soil, the students who are ripe for this information, who can make it work in their lives. The educator's role is to be the farmer going out to sow the seed, and we have developed many methods over the years to sow this seed in great quantities: twelve years of religious education, now enhanced with great delivery systems, such as modern communications and computers. But quantitative exposure to religious information isn't enough. It becomes too easy to rejoice that one-quarter of our farmland (that is, our young people) are growing and to dismiss the fact that three-quarters of the young people in our religious education programs cannot identify a personal relationship with Jesus or don't bother to worship with the community on Sunday, or both.

The exceptional parishes with a large percentage of youth worshiping with the rest of the community, will tell you they have done far more with their youth than present them with religious information. The programs in these parishes emphasize relationships, especially between students and teachers, and also between students and each other, teachers, parents, peers at school, brothers and sister, and the rest of the world. People who put an emphasis on relationships in religious growth would see the parable of the sower quite differently than people whose sole involvement is the transfer of information would.

Educators with a more relational view would see this parable as follows. The sower is the Father in heaven who flings the seed to earth (Jesus), who arrives upon the earth (through the Incarnation), with our lives as the soil. The seed, then, is not information, but the person of Jesus. Education is not the process of seed-flinging—heaving our information at our students in ever-increasing quantities, hoping something happens and dismissing the results when nothing does. Instead, as ministers we work the soil, plowing it, opening it, preparing it, weeding it, taking out the rocks (healing). But once growth is apparent, then cultivating the soil has to become our priority, as we care for the new growth, rejoicing in the dynamic of seed and soil in relationship.

As we shall see later in the section on evangelization and catechesis, preparing the soil before growth, before the Lord's tangible activity, is a different skill than is cultivating the soil after the Lord's activity becomes apparent in the individual's life. Preparing the soil, when we are confident that the Father will sow as promised, is an act of faith on our part, an event called evangelization, as we extend this promise of relationship to the people we meet who are not yet conscious of the Lord's activity in their lives. Cultivating the soil, when we are mindful of the activity of the Lord now becoming tangible, is an event we call catechesis, working with the Lord and clarifying his activity, his love, his guidance in the life of the individual.

It is obvious that most of our young people avoid or barely tolerate nonrelational information transfer programs. The shift toward relational education and formation is happening because the world is changing, because people need help with their relationships more than ever before, and because our theology shines when it is presented as a way of developing good experiences with others, as well as healing the bad experiences.

Our theology excites people when they discover we can actually have a personal relationship with Jesus, the God-Human who is incarnate within us, offering us the love that makes any relationship work.

So in the church's shift toward relational growth, the whole person is back in proper focus. The goal of these programs and exercises is not winning anything: not grades, not games, not even heaven. We don't need to win at the cost of someone else losing. Didn't the Crusades teach us this? We don't have to conquer anything but our own fears; we don't have to defeat anything but our hesitation in letting the Lord love us. The new relational goal will feature teamwork, discipline, and coordination of our spirit and body with what Jesus is doing in the body of Christ: the seed growing in more and more good soil.

What seems to be returning to the center of the church's ministry to youth, or anyone else, is an integrated approach that combines knowledge and activity and emphasizes building and sustaining relationships with God, others, and self. One teacher in a classroom isn't enough. One preacher in the pulpit isn't enough. One parent in the home isn't enough. One catechism or textbook isn't enough. To proclaim a kingdom of love featuring the abiding power and presence of God, we must proclaim with our whole person, not just with our mouths, that this love comes to us through relationships and returns to God through relationships. If education helps this, great. If preaching helps this, great. If any program, prayer group, or ceremony can help this, great.

In our return to the original Christian community model, we are rediscovering our roots, the dynamic love that made the early Christians so attractive and so dangerous (almost 300 years of persecution). In our return to meeting and sharing the Lord in our personal interaction, we discover that the classroom-teacher, the coach-teacher, the parent-teacher, and the celebrant-teacher aren't the only teachers. Everyone in the classroom, on the team, in the family, or in the worshiping community has something to share, something to teach. And as others tell the stories of their experiences of God and their encounters with others, revealing their own appreciation of themselves, then what is revealed is not just data or technique, but people, and within these people

God. Along the way what is revealed by God is the love we need to be happy: love that doesn't have to be won by our efforts, because it's a free gift; a love that we don't have to go to distant places to find, because it's within us, placed by God as a fulfillment of the promise, the covenant; a love that we can keep within us, and between us.

In our ministry to people, especially young people, any process is only a tool. The real goal is to reveal by our lives as well as with our words God's vital invitation to anyone we meet: to the quick and to the slow, to the agile and to the clumsy, to the popular and to the outcast, to the pious and to the impious, to the good soil and to the hardened, weedy, or rocky soil alike: the sower is throwing the seed. The kingdom of love is here. The Lord is here. All the love you'll ever need is here. Emmanuel: "God with us" (Matt. 1:23).

4. Images: The Way We Perceive and Communicate

It should be apparent that if God is love, then religion is relationships—relationships with God, with others, and with self. Religious tradition is a summary of past experiences people have had with God and with each other. It also includes the learning statements these people have gathered as a result of these experiences. In Catholic Christianity, tradition is both written and oral. Written Tradition is known as the sacred scriptures, the Bible, the Old and New Testaments, or the Hebrew and Christian scriptures. As understood by Christians, it is the written summary of significant religious experiences, with the major conclusions drawn from these experiences intended to be passed on (*traditio: "handed across"*) to succeeding generations for guidance. The experiences, the selection of which experiences to write down, and the conclusions that will be presented as teaching are all inspired by God. The same holds true for the Oral Tradition, the ongoing experiences and conclusions that first of all generated written tradition and have continually gathered even after the Written Tradition ended around the year 100 A.D.

The Oral Tradition is usually presented as dogmas or doctrines, sometimes including morality. But it can also be understood to include the stories of God and his people that occur every day: stories that are passed on by word of mouth. Of course, because of the power of religious fervor, some of these stories can be fashioned more out of the imagination than from fact, so the church claims the right to determine which major stories are factual and which stories are not. Sometimes this determination takes centuries.

So although thousands of stories of faith experiences are told daily in prayer groups, on retreats, between friends, through preaching, in books, on radio and television, and in liturgies featuring faith sharing, those stories remain in the preliminary vault of church experience and are seen as personal experiences, but not necessarily the official teaching of the church. Some of these experiences may continually be retold as important stories, with significant conclusions drawn by groups of people as a teaching worth passing on. But only after a great deal of time has elapsed will some of these stories be examined for their factual basis, and still more time and examination is required before the teaching or tradition value of these experiences will be announced and the stories integrated into the official teaching, consistent with already accepted facts and teaching. More often than not, many of the facts are lost during the retelling of these experiences, and the teaching conclusions are colored by the agendas of various religious groups and political entities, so the experiences are far more beneficial to their own goals than they are helpful to the whole church. Only a few experiences will survive all of this scrutiny to become dogmas; and only the teachings that remain consistent with already accepted teaching (or, at least, don't contradict past teaching) and are seen by church authorities as valuable for the whole church to hear will be presented as doctrine (teaching).

Within the Church, it is also worth noting, there is Tradition (capital *T*) and tradition (small *t*). The Church's Tradition, written and oral, is the summary of the experiences and teachings that always were and are and always will be available to people as truth.

On the other hand, many of the church's traditions are valuable to many Christians as local customs that aid in understanding and sharing faith for a period of time in the church's history, but were not central to the church's experience and may not be effective traditions during another period of church history.

Tradition (with a capital *T*) includes Jesus as an historical person; his life-giving gospel; the apostolic community; God's unconditional love for everyone; death and resurrection; eternal life; Jesus' power and presence with all nations.

However, traditions (with a small *t*) include some customs

and practices that are often thought to be part of Tradition but that, in fact, have existed during only a certain period in church's experience. So the Latin mass, the election of the pope by the college of cardinals, the rosary, novenas, and so on are all traditions. As long as these traditions help us understand and share our experiences of God and each other, they should remain. When they are no longer helpful, they will pass away and be replaced by more helpful traditions.

If God remains the same and people's needs are basically the same, then why is there a difference between Tradition and tradition? Why are there several rites and many denominations within Christianity? Why are there religious groups with "facts" at odds with Christian Tradition?

How can people experience and pray to the same God and then come away with different teachings? How can religious people go to war against other religious people, killing one another over which is the right way to explain God? How can people torture and condemn to death other people who say their understanding of God is different from the official teaching?

If there is only one God, then the only answer to these questions is that the ways we *perceive* this God must be different, and the ways we *share* our perceptions must be different. Human perceptions and our sharing of what we perceive are accomplished through *Images*. We can't know without images, and we can't share what we know without images. So accurate images are vital to any experience, expecially our religious experiences.

There is a famous parable of three blind men who encountered a tame elephant. (We know the elephant was tame because it didn't stomp them flat for what they did to it!) In examining what they found, one blind man held the trunk of the elephant and perceived it to be hairy and pliable, with a moist air passage at one end and tusks and a wet tongue at the other. Meanwhile, the second blind man had stumbled up against one of the legs and found it hairy, muscular, and sporting something like toenails at the bottom. The third blind man grabbed the tail and experienced its ropelike quality. All three men began to tell the story of their experience. They had heard from a bystander that what they had encountered was an elephant—the same elephant. But in their description of their experience, they began to argue over just what an elephant was. Each had *part* of the elephant, but thought he had encountered *all* of it. No agreement was ever reached, and the three remained blind in more ways than one.

One problem with perception is that we may think we have experienced all of something or someone when in fact we have only experienced part. What we do experience is real, but not total. What we contact may be true, but the conclusions can be partly false. If the blind men had only shared what they had experienced, they would have come to a more complete mental picture of an elephant, but still wouldn't have total knowledge of the elephant. Even with more sensitivity, more time, and the full use of their senses, and even if they could consult a team of elephant experts, they still wouldn't know all about that elephant, and they certainly wouldn't be able to know all about every elephant in the world. But at least a shared dialogue would have expanded the knowledge and prevented a fight.

If only Christians, and people of other religious perceptions, would learn the same lesson! If we could share our experiences and test them for fact, we also could expand our knowledge of God and prevent fights and divisions.

But even among people of good will, there is a need to perceive and share our perceptions using Images. Because an image is the mental picture our minds carry away from an encounter with something or someone, we can store knowledge of that experience after the encounter is over. We walk away with an image. The problem is that images have some limitations. And so do experiences. Since I can never experience a total object all at once from the same point of view, my experience of that item is limited. (Try it. Pick up any object, and try to see all of it from only one point of view. If you move it or turn it, you are changing the point of view.)

Now take the limited experience and store it in your mind, using an image that is also limited. You may have selected an image that doesn't match the experience, or the item you experienced may change, leaving your once-accurate image no longer accurate!

Because knowing God, and people around us, and even ourselves, is so vital to our spiritual growth, then images will play a significant role in the way we perceive God, others, and ourselves. Sometimes these images will help; sometimes they may get in the way.

Knowledge itself is simply a means to connect with God, a way of perceiving. Knowledge alone cannot be salvation. But knowing plays a major role in relationships. *What* we know is not nearly as important as *whom* we know.

Who is God? Who are the others in my life? Who am I? These are the questions whose answers not only tell us about someone; they tell us if we are loved, cared for, valued. Other information—dates, times, numbers, successes, failures, how tos—can only enhance the fact that we're loved. If we don't feel loved, if we don't know we're loved, and if we don't know who loves us, then the whats, wherefores, how manys and how tos become distractions, leading us to the data of religion, but not the meaning. Information about God then becomes only a substitute for personal knowledge of God, the church, Jesus Christ, and the love that calls us from our loneliness. The Scribes and Pharisees felt the anger of Jesus because they had used information and the law to materialize religion into a code of doing holy things, but they weren't holy. They were just "whitened sepulchres, full of dead men's bones" (Matt. 23:27). Pious practices; no meaning.

As we have seen, there is a major difference between knowing about someone and personally knowing that person. I can listen to several people tell me about you. And, depending on their objectivity, their biases, their perceptions, their images, and their ability to communicate all of that into my images—all of which are influenced by subjective forces in me—I may learn something about you.

But until we meet person to person, I won't be in direct contact with you, and I cannot claim to know you. I can hear enough about you to "feel like I know you," as you have no doubt heard people say. But until we've met, we really don't know each other. Meeting one another doesn't always guarantee we will get to know each other, because we might be playing games, hiding from each other. But a direct encounter always offers the best opportunity to know one another.

Over the years we have come up with much information about God, about church, about society, about friendship, about psychology, and, especially, about love. But who wants to be fully educated about a God whom you will never meet in this life? Who wants the theology and history of the church, when everyday contact reveals that no one seems to know or care for one another? Who wants a church study group on friendship if all this group does is publish a new and expanded list of warnings? Who needs another morality course specializing in avoiding relationships?

I remember several courses in morality in relationships throughout my religious education. It always seemed to me that these courses could be summed up in a word: "No!" All the books we used in these courses included the word *morality* in the title, but from the first page to the end of the book, we were shown all the things that could go wrong in our relationships, all the ways we could sin, even the various kinds of sin. We were shown how to avoid the act of sin, how to avoid the near occasion of sin, and the three conditions of sin (is it a seriously sinful action, do you know it's serious, do you freely choose to perform the action). When we finished every morality course, I had the feeling that I knew more about sin, more about cutting myself off from God, and more about confession than I did about loving properly, which is the true definition of morality. In fact, in all of my years in Catholic schools, including the seminary, I never had a course in living, in handling my relationships properly, in dealing effectively with feelings, in learning to express my feelings appropriately, in helping to heal relationships I had damaged. I realize now that those courses and textbooks were misnamed. Instead of *Morality*, they should have been named *Immorality*, because that's what they were all about. Where today can you find a morality course that teaches what it claims to teach: loving properly?

If we experience and accept God's unconditional love for us, we are saved from loneliness, from isolation from God, and from confusion about our worth. And if we pass on that same love to others, we are ministering: calling others to experience the love we have come to know as God. And if we love properly, if we care appropriately about the people we meet, and if we love ourselves by accepting the appropriate love of others and live growth-centered lives, then we are moral.

The best way to know God and other people is through direct, personal contact. Once we are in contact directly with someone, then other people's descriptions about the same person can enhance our awareness, or challenge it to expand. The same holds true in our relationship with God. As we develop our one-to-one relationship with God, other people can share their experiences, their stories, and expand our understanding of God, and maybe even challenge our awareness to grow. This "telling our story" of our God-experiences is called faith sharing and is an indispensable means of spiritual growth. You tell your stories; I'll tell mine. Sometimes our stories are radically different; sometimes similar. But all of these stories reveal God in some way. God moves in many disguises, and in many images, and is in every life—somewhere. Many needs. Many experiences. One faith. One Lord.

It's all so simple, until we use those images. As we make contact with anyone, our process of knowing involves using images. These pictures in our mind display our impressions of ourselves and others, including God. Whether we gather these images directly from the relationship or indirectly through others; stories and teachings, we will come away from that contact with some idea of the person or situation involved.

Sometimes our images are accurate; sometimes not. A lot depends on our prejudices, our openness, our previous experiences, our willingness to change our images to fit reality, and our sense of self-worth. Usually, though, direct contact with the person or situation gives us the best chance of forming an accurate image. On the other hand, when direct contact does not help, we may need intervention from someone we trust and who can challenge us to face reality. How many times has a friend challenged our biased perception of someone and urged us to see that person more accurately?

As we grow in any relationship, our original images may expand or even change dramatically. If this change moves us closer to an accurate understanding of another, then we call it growth. As we become more accurately revealed to ourselves and to others, then we're also growing. All of this takes place through images. We not only actually change; our images of ourselves and other change, too. Our spiritual and mental health and growth can be measured by our accuracy in forming and reforming images of an objective reality and then responding appropriately.

God is. Friends are. I am. These are facts (reality). But if I misunderstand these persons, then I have a perception problem, an image problem. I remember one kid in school who always seemed to bug me. For years I carried a negative image of this kid, until the year our desks were adjoining. You already know that I was very creative as a youngster, especially when I was bored. But until this other classmate moved next to me, I didn't know how good I could be on a team! We became partners in creative distraction and good friends in the process. Until I had found a quality in him I respected, I couldn't appreciate his delightful and complementary differences. Once I discovered something in him that challenged my past image, I was willing to construct a whole new relationship!

We use images in all forms of perception and communication. Teaching uses images. Music uses images. This book uses images. Jesus uses images. I use them; my friends use them; the church uses them. Everywhere people communicate what they know with images, after first learning what they know through images. In my theology classes I used to drive my professors crazy by questioning everything. It's not that I doubted what they were teaching; I just needed to translate their images into images I could understand. Sometimes my sets of images weren't adequate to handle what they were saying, and I had to change them to deal with the facts. Sometimes my questions stretched their images a little bit too, but to their credit, our dialogues continued without interruption, although certain professors were never able to hide a look of trepidation as my hand once more flew into the air!

One time in the seminary, shortly after the word came from Rome to turn the main altars around so the priest could face the people, we walked into our chapel for mass and noticed that the main altar had been moved from the back wall and positioned much closer to the students' pews. This was the seminary rector's response to the liturgical reforms that were coming out of Vatican II. I believe ours was the first sanctuary in that diocese to undergo this rearrangement. And the rector was to be admired for his responsiveness.

As the mass began, however, we could see that the rector's hand gestures were still in what seminarians fondly referred to as the robot position and his eyes were lowered throughout this new face-to-face liturgy. It became obvious that the personal reforms were going to be much slower than the physical changes. So I stopped by the rector's room later that day to share my impressions of the new look. I complimented him on the new altar arrangement, but as my ulterior motives steered the conversation toward his liturgical posture, I heard myself saying, "Father, when the seminary students get out of line in their behavior, we have the faculty to correct us, right?"

Crisp answer: "Right."

I plowed ahead, "And when the faculty get out of line, they have the rector to correct them, right?"

Even crisper: "Right."

I could feel myself arriving at one of those "meaning of life" moments in our relationship. Our eyes locked, and I bleated, "Who corrects the rector?"

His eyes, still locked on mine, became two drills minus the novocaine. He asked, "What did you have in mind?"

I brashly noted that the liturgical reforms were implemented to regain the dialogical nature of worship: God and people as well as people and people, with a renewed emphasis on community and interaction. And in view of that, it would be good if the contact between the celebrant and the rest of the community could be increased in every way possible. "It would really be helpful," I concluded, sightless as his optical drills continued to work on my discomfort nerve, "if you would open your eyes and communicate with us during liturgy."

His response was classically Roman: "Young man, I have been saying mass this way for fifteen years, and I have no intention of changing."

I know I also heard a growl, but I didn't see his mouth move. Again I bleated, "Just thought I'd mention it. Sorry if I've bothered you." I exited.

The next morning, his eyes were open.

We had communicated. Two sets of images had collided. Two flawed, sincere, and caring people had changed and grown from our contact. I won't forget that moment, and probably neither will he. We were bigger at that moment than our images, and in the contact we had made, it became possible to criticize and to change. And possible to become friends.

Even something as spiritual as a thought or a feeling between friends still requires imaging through words, gestures, or sounds. When two people come into contact with the same object, each will probably use different images to describe it. As our three blind men can testify, one object can seem like different objects after we hear the various descriptions.

When it is vitally important to agree on using a common image, then many experiences must first be sifted for the facts and much dialogue must take place, featuring all of the different points of view. This process is usually accompanied by a certain amount of tension. Look at all the church councils down through the centuries, as Christians from many cultures and worshiping communities, each with their own sets of images, gathered together to come to an understanding of Jesus, the Eucharist, the meaning of salvation, the communion of saints, and so on. Certainly the people who gathered at each of those councils had faith, experienced God, and spoke with an urgency on many issues involving faith and ministry. Why the struggle? Why the intensity? Images! You see it one way; I see it another. How will we present our conclusions in one image the whole church can understand?

Especially when it comes to understanding God, there will be many points of view, many accurate ways of understanding God, explaining God, and worshiping God. Jesus, who is the word of God made flesh, is presented in the Christian scriptures (New Testament) in forty-three different images: Son of God, Suffering Servant, Messiah, and so on. Maybe God knows our image problems and offers plenty of accurate images for everyone! You find one or two of those images particularly helpful as you try to perceive and reveal your experience of God. Fine! I may find a couple of others helpful for me. Let's not fight. Let's share, and listen to one another.

Even as we change and respond to God and to others around

us, our images will change. An adult will find childhood images inadequate to perceive society, responsibilities, friendship, God, others, and even self. As we change, our images need to keep up. As society changes, the church must keep pace, without giving up anything essential. Some imagery is negotiable; some isn't. The Tradition will not be negotiable, but the tradition will be. We can change our expressions of faith as needed, but cannot change the fact of God's availability through the Incarnation and God's love for us.

Everyone has an image of God, accurate or not. Over your lifetime, possibly hundreds of images of God have been presented to you by teachers, parents, clergy, friends, movies, songs, coloring books, Bible stories, nonbelievers, and even antibelievers. At different times in your life, you have found particular images of God helpful. Maybe you've gone through a whole set of favorite images, but at this point in your life you operate with one image that works best for you. It may seem that your parents or teachers *taught* you one memorable image but, in fact, they only presented you images. At some point you selected, or agreed to, your image, one that clicks for you.

This image has become your primary image of God. Christians have their forty-three images of Christ, for example. But individual Christians usually have only one primary image when they visualize Jesus. And each image is slightly different from another in detail, even when believers select the same image. Non-Christian believers also have their images of God, and even atheists have an image of God that they've rejected ("I don't believe in a God who permits war and lets babies die"). So everyone has a primary image of God.

And your image of God will affect your image of Jesus Christ. You even use your image of God to support your image of Christ. Just listen to Christians discuss different notions of Jesus, and when things start to heat up, someone will eventually defend a view by saying: "Well, God says . . . " And that "God" will curiously always say just the right thing to support the image of Christ under discussion.

To make things more complicated, your image of Christ will affect your image of the church. Again, listen to Christians talking about what the church ought to be like, what should be corrected about it, and so on, and you're going to hear "Well, Jesus said . . . ," as the convincing argument.

And finally, your image of the church will affect your concept of ministry. Isn't ministry what the church does? Then it will be consistent with your understanding of the church.

It all goes back to your notion of God, taken from direct experience or from the indirect experience of being taught by someone else. And, I believe, your reason for selecting one image over all the others as your primary image of God is that it matches your self-image. It works well in relationship to the way you see yourself.

Do you really think your religious training made you select your primary image of God? Lots of attractive and lots of scary images were drilled into you by your parents and teachers. But you picked one of those, or discovered a new one they hadn't mentioned, as your current image of God. And your images of Jesus, the church, and ministry all fit accordingly with that image of God. And your key image of God relates perfectly to your image of yourself.

One time I was counseling a twenty-year-old about a religious problem he was having, and he kept coming back to the notion that he had done so many bad things in his life that God couldn't possibly want to forgive and love him. He thought the things he had done were unforgivable! His image of God was as the Judge, and he was guilty. He just knew God saw all that bad stuff and was keeping a book on him. And when he talked about Jesus Christ, he could only talk about the cross and all the suffering Jesus had to endure because of sinners like him. In fact, he took personal responsibility for killing Jesus Christ with his sins. Now that's guilt! Connected with that image was his image of the church. Because he was a sinner, everyone else probably was too. And sinners have to be reminded how bad they are and how they had better shape up, or else God, who had already lost his son over this, was going to let everyone really have it! So why wasn't the church getting tough with those people in the pews? What good was all this lovey-dovey stuff? Let's get back to the basics: sin. Let's remind people of their basic sinfulness, show them how bad they are, and then maybe we can motivate them to accept God's unfathomable gift of ultimate forgiveness. And if people didn't realize they're all sinners (as he had) and do something about it, then they were all going to hell, where unrepentant sinners must go. In his view the church needed more of this tough preaching, along with some more laws to keep those sinners under control. Law and order, that's what the church needed! And to enforce this system of law and order, and to teach and preach this system, we needed people who were holier, people who were clearly in charge, people with a special character on their souls who were visibly set apart from the sinning throng: people in uniform. We needed more priests, more nuns, more brothers; and we must get them back into their clerical dress! To this young man, the ministry of the church meant enforcing the gospel, getting essentially sinful people to become repentant, saving them from hell, reminding them that an angry God was willing to take them back. But the ministry of the church was the call of God to the few; to enter the ministry meant being set apart by way of life and uniform for this special work.

Remember, this is an image of God, Christ, the church and ministry all built around this person's own self-image. And yet we would have to agree that in both the scriptures and in the practices of the church similar imagery abounds. For him, it all fit together. But he was unhappy, and that's why he had come to see me. The only way out of this feeling, as he saw it, would, be to accept the overwhelming fact of his guilt, seek forgiveness, and hope that God would agree to forgive him. Then he should leave behind his way of life and his temptations and enter the priesthood, thereby finding closeness with God. This would appease this angry God and bring peace to his tortured soul, as well as place him in a disciplined way of life with a distinctive role. Then he could help others change their sinful way of life.

This may have been his image of the solution to the problem when he first came in for counseling. It wasn't the solution we reached together after many visits, I can assure you. Let me just say that he is much happier today, and all of his images have changed, especially his self-image. As his self-image has changed, he has been amazed to find that his images have also changed regarding God, Christ, the church, and ministry. He is

finding peace of soul, and he sees himself as much closer to
God and even finds God much more approachable now that he
isn't so afraid of him. He didn't have to leave his life behind to
find God. Instead he has discovered God right where he has
been living all along. As he found himself to be a good place to
live, he realized that God had long ago found him to be an acceptable temple for his power and presence. As the rest of his
images have expanded and multiplied, he claims to have a better grip on reality (perception) and much better relationships
with others (perception and sharing).

I've dealt with other people who operated with a different
set of images. One person I remember well saw herself as basically a loved person. She knew she wasn't perfect, but she was
loved anyway and could still grow in the areas of her life that
were weak. This well-adjusted young woman saw God as a
friend, someone with whom she could carry on a dialogue
comfortably. For her, Jesus became man to reveal this love to
her, a love that took the form of forgiveness whenever she
made mistakes, even serious ones. And this forgiveness was always offered. All she had to do was accept it and grow from the
experience. She found Jesus constantly available to reveal new
ways to grow and sensed him as the person who lived within
her and within the people around her. As she saw it, those who
know they're loved (through faith) gather as a community to
share their experiences of this loving God (faith sharing), who
remains present and visible in their midst and whose power
works through them. This God-in-us is Jesus Christ, working
within the community to invite deeper recognition and growth
and also working from the same community to touch others. As
the people of the faith community agree to allow this power to
work through them and as this community called the church
sees its mission more clearly, then the believers can take responsibility not only to "love one another," but to love especially those outside the community who don't know of this incredible love, who don't know Jesus, whose power and
presence is available to them too. For this young woman, this
was the ministry of the church. All of her images fit together,
although they were still flexible. At this point in her life, she
saw herself as happy. She knew that the images operating in

her life gave her a solid perception and a grip on reality, and through her interaction with others she shared her perception. And she understood how to communicate with others: find out what images they are using and try to work within those images. She knew what images worked best for her, but she also was wise enough to know that others might use different images.

The key, then, seems to be the self-image. And your self-image will dictate all of your compatible images as you construct your view of the world around you. This self-image will affect your selection of friends, spouse, job, peer group, clothes, music, way of life, and even values. Each of your selections will be made from many options, but must coordinate with your self-image. Aren't you unhappy when reality doesn't fit with your view of the world? Would you rather change the world than change your images? Would you rather change God than allow God to change you? Do you want God to see the way you see and do what you think needs to be done? Or will you allow yourself to see reality with the eyes of God?

When your image structure becomes a theory of life that forces reality to fit your images—like a person squeezing into clothing that is too small—then "the fit won't fit." The facts don't match the image, so you spend the rest of your days trying to change reality, leaving you deeply dissatisfied. Or you change the images you use, growing in the process and becoming a person who deals effectively with reality. It's been my experience that the closer I am in touch with reality, the closer I am to God, to myself, and to others.

A German professor, during the nineteenth century, was presenting his theory of life to his students. At one point in the presentation, a student asked, "Professor, what happens if a fact is discovered that destroys your theory?" The professor answered, using the Latin of the university, "*Pereat Factum*": Let the fact perish!

We would rather cling to our images than allow them to change. And the image we would rather not change at all is our self-image, because our worldview is linked to our self-view. I find reasons to dislike others, or try to change them, beacuse they conflict with my perceptions, my images. But when crises, or deep relationships, or personal conversion experiences happen to me, my view of myself can change. And as these opportunities challenge my self-image to grow and become more effective, my compatible images will be challenged as well.

Wise people know that there are only three changes we can try to make in our lives. We can try to change others, influencing them constructively or destructively to become what we want them to be. Second, we can also try to change our environment, which could involve moving to another place or rearranging some of the "furniture" around us. This can prove very helpful as long as the new arrangement keeps us in contact in reality. Often, however, this can be used to distract us from dealing with serious problems, leaving us "shuffling the deck chairs on the Titanic." Third, we can change ourselves. This is where we have the most control, as well as the most opportunities. If everything isn't perfect, we can still grow. Even if the world around us seems intolerable, we can still grow. We no longer have to be people waiting for conditions to be right for us. We can still change ourselves, and a good portion of that changing will happen in the way we perceive ourselves, others, and God, or in the ways we choose to love ourselves, others, and God. As we change, our images will have played a major role in our finding new ways to perceive and love.

As we learn to see ourselves and the world around us with the eyes of God, as we see God at work in this world with the eyes of faith, and as we join God in his work of loving the people of this world, we will be the church in the best sense. We will be experiencing the excitement of discovering our own beauty and knowing that God doesn't make junk. And we can be telling the world that we know from our own experience that the forgiveness of God, when accepted, releases us from guilt, so that we can see who we really are. The worst thing about guilt is that it distracts us from our own beauty. So of course God wants guilt removed!

Because images play a crucial role in people's growth, the church has a tremendous responsiblity as custodian of the power and presence of Jesus Christ. As a result, the church must constantly monitor the world's images and be alert to people's systems of knowledge and perception. Because any perception of reality is filtered and maintained through images, it is important that the best possible set of images be used to present the facts of religion. But this is never easy. Who has decided which is the best set of images for a culture? Who has monitored the relationsip of images to reality, making sure that images remain clear and helpful and true?

Who has translated the facts of religion into many tongues, as at Pentecost? Who has advised the world which translations have illuminated the facts, rather than compromised them for a particular culture?

Who has agreed that some truth exists in all religions, and at the same time has challenged each religion and denomination to conduct a dialogue and to clarify its truth?

Who has announced that God's revelation has two integrated ways of imaging the truth: Written Tradition and Oral Tradition?

So, although the church seems a bit slow in studying and defining new images, and as religious warnings seem to be flying everywhere in the church, remember this: the responsibility for accurate definition is huge. And proper balance is always delicate. But the church claims this responsibility.

Yet in some periods of history, the church did not wait for science, technology, art, or way of life to present facts or images for the church's review. The church took the lead in presenting its own understanding of truth through art, music, theater, way of life, and languages. The monasteries, the universities, and especially the Renaissance are good examples.

Today, however, it appears that the church has all it can handle in responding to new facts, techniques, ways of life, and images presented by people and institutions around the world. Because of the sheer volume of issues raised in a modern world, the process of responding requires both openness and caution.

When the church demands that an older system of images remain as the accepted tool of understanding, then the church appears to be conservative. What this means is that the newer images don't seem to improve on what we already have.

When the church demands that a society, even the church itself, change its system of images and operational codes, then the church appears to be liberal.

Generally, the church appears to be more conservative on dogmatic and doctrinal issues and in the area of personal morality. But in the issues of civil morality and social justice, the church seems to be more liberal.

Remember, though, that history has shown that when the church says "No" to some dogmatic, doctrinal, or moral perspective, this "No" might mean anything from "We will never change on this" to "Hold on! We're studying this, but cannot recommend it right now." And knowing the church's response is like knowing another person: the better you know that person, the better you know his or her moods, hurts, excitement, and especially what he or she means when saying "no."

5. Original Sin and the Task of the Ministry—Two Notions

In our search for happiness, we can look many places. We can seek happiness in material things, in the conquest or the avoidance of others, in drugs or alcohol, but we can ultimately never be happy unless we have someone to love us unconditionally and forever. This love will, of course, be valuable to us only if we agree to be loved, choosing freely to accept this gift.

These are the ingredients brought together in religion. In every religious story we see people who are lonely and people who have been saved from isolation by allowing themselves to be loved completely. In short, God is the fulfillment of our needs. He is the reason we search and the goal of our search. But God, like any good friend, does not want to force his love upon us. So, besides the gift of existence and the gift of his permanent offer of love, we have another gift that guarantees that we can choose whether we want to be in a relationship with God: the gift of free will. Its highest purpose is to allow us to make this choice: do I want to be loved permanently and unconditionally by God? Whichever way I choose, there are consequences.

In the Judeo-Christian tradition all ingredients of this choice are brought together in the story of Adam and Eve. This account is about God's offer and the choice two people made in response. We know about God's face-to-face encounters with Adam and Eve, and the ease of that relationship at first, as well as the beautiful environment in which they lived. And then we see their decision to live without God, to be independent. And finally, we see the results of the choice: the consequences of choosing to be free from God instead of free with God.

This original use of free will to separate from God is called original sin. But what was the main consequence of this sin? In separating from God, what happened to Adam and Eve? And what happened to us? Was there any real damage? And if there was, can it be repaired? How?

Unfortunately, the church is divided on the exact effect original sin had on Adam and Eve, and has on us. There are, however, two main schools of thought, each of which has developed its own salvation task, based on its point of view.

It must seem strange that the church can be divided on so important an issue, but this is currently the case. With two views on the effects of original sin, we have two views on the effects of being saved, and, of course, two views on the tasks of ministry.

We find evidence of these two perspectives in the early Christian communities, as well as throughout the Christian experience down through the centuries, although each has worn different labels over the years. These theologies—each with its own images of humanity, each with a specific vision of the work God is doing to save humanity—may look to outsiders as if the church doesn't really know what it's doing. And because of these diverging theologies, groups of Christians have clashed on the battlefield, argued in councils, and jostled each other on the ministry trail.

This is not just a casual debate over the consequences of original sin. To start with, both groups agree on the basic goodness of all creation before original sin. What God creates is essentially good, and goodness is part of the very nature of all creation. Both groups agree that the peak of the creation experience is man and woman, "made in God's own image" (Gen. 1:27), playing a special role in God's plan to have what he has begun brought somehow to a satisfactory completion, with the happiness of the human race foremost in his mind.

Both groups agree on a unique quality given only to man and woman: free will. This incredible gift allows us to use our reflective consciousness in analyzing options and making choices, especially choices that will affect our happiness. We are able to make choices that take us beyond our animal instincts. But we might make choices that can harm our chances of finding genuine happiness. And it's a risk for God as well as for us. What if someone uses this power against him? Or against others? Or against themselves? In other words, for human beings to use this power properly in making the right choices, they also have the freedom to make the wrong choices. So free will is a gift that is loaded with risk.

And yet, despite the risk, God has given us that gift. We will not be puppets, with God as the Great Puppeteer who dangles us on strings, merely pretending that we can make real choices.

With this gift we become part of God's plan, free to love, free to refuse to love. Either way we choose, there will be consequences. That's why choices are made: to produce consequences. If the good consequences outweigh the bad ones, then the choice was a good one. If the bad consequences outweigh the good ones, then the choice was a bad one. But what is good and what is bad? Because differences of opinion will exist on what is objectively good and bad, God will involve himself in the process and guide us in our choices. But this guidance will never revoke our power to choose once the guidance has taken place. God will not revoke his gift of free will, even to spare us the consequences of our choice.

Both theological groups in this debate agree that before original sin, the first man and first woman shared an intimate closeness with God, conversing easily and frequently with him. There was a clarity to the relationship, a face-to-face ease with him. But for God, this comfort and ease with one another needed one more ingredient for it to be honorable for man and woman; they should buy into it themselves, using their free will to do that for which this gift was created. For a complete relationship, both sides should freely agree to participate and grow together. In effect, God said, "And so, man and woman, do you want to know only what's good, which will include our intimacy together? Or would you like to know good and evil? You have the power—your power—to choose."

Finally, both groups agree that man and woman chose to know good and evil, exercising their gift to select an option that they thought would make them like God. That choice was most unfortunate, if you will permit an understatement, because man and woman already had all the goodness they could experience. They had God, face-to-face. They had each other. They had all of creation. All of that was essentially good. In eating of the tree of knowledge of good and evil, they were adding to their knowledge only the second part, evil, and in choosing this knowledge, they were to receive what they chose. They would now know evil as fully as they had known good.

It is at this point that the two groups part trails, unable to agree on the actual consequence of the choice. In choosing to know good and evil, was goodness destroyed, thereby making humanity basically evil? Did God remove his power and presence from the world, or merely allow evil to hide it, letting evil coexist with goodness? How you answer these questions will place you within one of the groups, and you will find yourself in conflict with the perceptions and the ministerial styles of the other group. It is to be hoped that you won't stop loving them, and you won't stop believing that God works through them to reach many people.

One group perceives that those born after the Fall are basically evil and without God. The ministry and theology of this group deals with humanity as basically evil, in need of salvation. I call this the Excarnational perspective. The other group perceives humanity as still basically good, with its gift of goodness still intact, but wounded and hidden from God by the evil that was chosen. Salvation is still necessary, but the process of salvation is seen in a different light than the first group view it. I call this the Incarnational perspective. Later in this chapter I will examine each perspective in greater detail.

If we remember that a perspective involves, as the word suggests, "seeing" a reality, or part of a reality, then we won't forget that this reality is filtered through the images we use. If our images are stitched together into our worldview, then events that happen outside of us are brought into our awareness and judged as either supporting and reinforcing our worldview, or challenging and contradicting it. Obviously, we prefer events to fit easily into our own perspective.

The part if our worldview that involves the way we perceive God is known as a theology: literally, the word about God. As we saw earlier, each of us has a major image of God, which connects to a consistent set of images of Christ, church, and ministry and must somehow also fit our self-image. Our total set of images makes up our perspective on God, so it becomes our theology, which also includes our view of people. If I think people are basically evil, then my theology will include the compatible view of God doing something in this world to save these people from their evil. On the other hand, if I view people as basically good, but doing some evil things, then my theology will see the work of God differently.

I honestly don't think God particularly cares which perspective we use, as long as we are in relationship with him and do our best to love others as we minister to them. As far as I can tell from my own relationship with God, he sees the world the way it really is, not filtered through limited images.

We, however, don't have that advantage. Our images can grow closer to the way God sees, as our own prayer-dialogues with God deepen our perspectives and expand them, but—at least in this life—we "still look at the world with some distortion, as in a reflection in a mirror, though later we shall see face-to-face" (1 Cor. 13:12). If our perspectives include prejudices and destructive biases, then we can expect the Lord to challenge these narrow images. When St. Paul was knocked to the ground on the road to Damascus, and later when something like scales fell from his eyes (Acts 9:4,18), he was the same person, but had a completely new perspective, a new view of reality. And the rest of his life was reoriented around his new theology. He began to work with and for Jesus Christ instead of persecuting his followers.

I don't think conversion of our lives and hearts to the Lord will mean necessarily crossing over from one perspective to the other. The Lord usually seems to allow us to remain within our same worldview, but he helps us see more, helps us expand some of our images and categories of knowing. True spiritual conversion is agreeing to permit the Lord love us, to be intimate with us, and to work through us to reach other people. Sometimes changing perspectives helps; sometimes it doesn't.

It won't take long to figure out which perspective or worldview I have. It will be more important for you to know which model you use, and to remember: either view or model can work. Our job is not to demand that people switch perspectives. If we call ourselves ministers of Jesus, then we love people in both models, just as the Lord does. If there is to be any change of perspective, the Lord will lead each person accordingly. Both perspectives, both theological models, have been around for 2,000 years in Christianity, and probably existed in some form before that, because they articulate the two major ways people seem to frame reality. History has shown us that people have gone to war and performed horrible atrocities in the service of their theology. We don't need any more of that. If we believe we must conquer someone to preach the gospel, then we really don't believe in the power and presence of Jesus Christ.

The Excarnational Perspective

During the creation of the world and the first man and first woman, God was deeply in love with this world and especially proud of the people he had made in his image. He saw that "it was good" (Gen. 1:31). This goodness was apparent during the conversations God had with this man and this woman. There was nothing between them but love.

Then man and woman made their choice for independence from God, and the result was . . . well, let's see.

The group that operates from what I call the Excarnational perspective believes that this basic goodness was destroyed. As a consequence of the sin of Adam and Eve (Gen. 3:6), this first man and first woman and all their descendants lost the goodness of their human nature and became evil. And because man and woman are evil, God cannot be present within them. God does not dwell in a place that isn't holy.

I call this perspective Excarnational because this worldview sees men and women as born *without* God, who stays outside the human condition because it is evil and the flesh is corrupt. *Excarnational*, in fact, literally means "outside the flesh." It is the perception that men and women begin their lives without God within them.

But God has not given up on humanity. Although he has withdrawn his presence and although his power is no longer easily available, he will send a Redeemer who will save us from our sins. This Redeemer will be seen as the "New Adam" (Rom. 5:15 and 1 Cor. 15:22) who will bring the power and presence of God back to men and women. In this theology salvation occurs through Jesus Christ, who is this New Adam, the Son of God in whom the power and presence rests.

When men and women recognize their evil nature, and see their condition without God, and when they repent and invite God back into their lives, then God will come into their lives, bringing with him his power and presence.

It should be noted that in this model we must agree to let God into our lives to be saved. If we don't invite God back, we remain without God and die without God, and then we will have to live eternally without God, in hell.

Once God does arrive (after we invite him), what takes place in us is again a matter of debate. Do we revert back to our original goodness? Does God restore our own goodness to us as he takes up his residence in us? One group says yes. Once God returns, our personal human nature becomes a "new creation" (2 Cor. 5:17), with all its original goodness. The old evil nature is destroyed, and the new nature is good as when the first man and first woman were created.

Another group, however, holds that when God comes into our lives, he is the only good within us. We are still evil, but we draw on the life of God within us. We are nothing and God is everything. God's continued presence substitutes for our lost goodness. So although we still possess no goodness of our own, God supplies what is needed as long as we sustain our relationship with him. Our full restoration does not occur until we arrive in heaven.

Although there is some disagreement on the consequences of salvation within the Excarnation perspective, there is unity on certain key elements: we must recognize our evil nature, and then invite God to come into our life. At that point God arrives to direct our lives, and if we remain faithful to his guidance, we will attain heaven ourselves and even help others find the same salvation.

The Incarnational Perspective

The Incarnational perspective is the view that despite original sin, our basic goodness was not ever destroyed. The goodness of our human nature was, however, weakened, wounded, and hidden from easy view. This is why Adam and Eve "hid" themselves from God and "covered" their bodily parts used to cocreate with God (Gen. 3:7).

We are still basically good, but the evil that the first man and first woman accepted into the human experience is now a veil that hides our goodness from us. We need to rediscover both our goodness and God, who lives within our goodness.

This perspective is called Incarnational because it sees men and women as born *with* God. God lives inside the human condition because it is still good, but remains hidden behind the veil of flesh, which is wounded, but not corrupt. Our human nature needs healing, but the healer, who awaits within, needs our agreement for the healing power and presence to have any effect.

So God is born into our human condition, arriving in our flesh (literally, *in carne*) to extend his invitation from within us, not above us or beyond us. God is here, now, waiting for our response.

Original sin, however, has weakened the intimacy with God that was so much a part of the relationship enjoyed by the first man and first woman. Once they chose independence, they began to experience evil, which competed with the goodness they had already known, and, in fact, began to hide that goodness from view. Instead of intimacy, they experienced a shadowy form of communication with God that left the participants talking to one another only through symbols, through a veil. After this sin the face of God is not revealed again until Jesus' arrival. Instead there is much hiding: man and woman hiding from God, hiding their nakedness; God veiled behind clouds, in a pillar of fire, in a burning bush, in the ark of the covenant; and then Jesus, concealed within our flesh, in our humanity, within us.

The Incarnational model features God in the flesh, revealed not only as Jesus Christ, but upon closer inspection, revealed also in us. God is already physically present in our lives, but there is no personal relationship until we agree to one. Until we accept his offer of love, we cannot grow in this love. And all along he remains veiled in the flesh of our humanity until he can be unveiled in the relationship to which he invites us.

The Incarnational perspective does not deny that there is

evil within us. But this evil has not replaced our original goodness, just hidden it. The power and presence of Jesus guarantees that God will always be available to us, closer to us than
we are to ourselves. Because the power of evil abuses us by hiding our goodness from us, the work of Jesus is to conquer that
evil by "uncovering what has lain hidden from the beginning"
(Matt. 13:35 quoting Ps. 78:2), by revealing what is behind the
veil of evil: our goodness, and his power and presence.

And because Jesus is the "Revelation of the Father's Love"
(John 15:9–10 and Rom. 8:39), then the mission of Jesus is not
to make us see how bad we are, but to see how good and how
loved we are. The work of revelation (from the Latin word *reve-
lare*, "to unveil") is to peel away the barriers. If Jesus is the revelation of God, then we have the chance of seeing what is behind the flesh: God in the flesh or Jesus Christ. Within our
own goodness is the continued power and presence of God.
Emmanuel means "God with us." The union of God and humanity, Jesus Christ, is "made not by the power of mankind, nor by
any human act, but by God Himself" (John 1:13).

In short, the Incarnational perspective sees the power and
presence of Jesus as a permanent part of us. In contrast to the
Excarnational view, there is no new arrival of God within us,
because he has been there all along. Instead, God invites *us* to
accept a relationship with him that will unveil even more of
his presence and release within us all the power of his kingdom. Because he respects us enough to take up his dwelling in
us, and because he believes in us enough to offer his power to
us, and because he values a two-way relationship with us, we
must use our own free will to "bring to completion the work
that is started within us" (Phil. 1:6). If we agree to this relationship with God, we will find and enjoy all the love we will ever
need, even in this life.

Jesus makes visible God's covenant, his offer for a permanent
relationship. He will be our God and we must agree to be his
people to complete the covenant (Exod. 24:3). But even if we
don't agree, he will still remain within us, offering his part of
the covenant, hoping that we will some day change our minds
and return to him, in a full relationship.

But the revelation doesn't stop there. God invites us to see and to reveal our goodness to others in our relationships with them. We are even invited to look behind the veil that hides others from us and even from themselves, and help reveal the "Kingdom at Hand" (Matt. 3:2), the kingdom within them as well. The revelation of God, others, and our true selves will all occur within our relationships.

Incarnational theology concludes that relationships are the field of ministry. Our relationships are also part of our salvation. As we interact with God, we see more than we did before. We come to know him as friend. We realize how loved we are, and at the same time see the need to tell others, show others, reveal to others the good news.

Salvation also requires an individual choice to allow the Lord to love us, which means that some kind of relationship between the individual and God needs to exist. Because the first man and first woman chose to be independent from God, each of us must choose to enter back into a relationship with God. God will not force the full relationship without our individual approval. What was veiled by a choice must be unveiled by a choice.

Salvation, therefore, occurs when God's invitation to a relationship, to friendship is accepted. And this invitation will constantly be offered during the individual's earthly life. And to be sure everyone hears this invitation, God offers it not from afar, not from heaven or from another galaxy, but from his own presence within each person, and between people in their relationships.

Short of taking back his gift of free will and forcing us to accept his love, God does everything possible to be available, to be clear about our options, to persuade without manipulating, and to call to us through our relationships, through the music around us, through the splendor of creation, in fact, through anything at which we look or to which we listen. But the choice must be ours.

The differences between these two perspectives should be clear by now. In the Excarnational model God leaves and then when we ask comes back into each of us. In the Incarnational model God never leaves, but remains within us and between us to be discovered and accepted.

The arrival of God, in the Excarnational perspective, is the salvation experience. In the Incarnational perspective, God is already present from the beginning of the person's life, and salvation is an ongoing series of deepening discoveries of his presence, and an ongoing series of yeses, leading to a more profound friendship with God. As this relationship develops, the power of the Lord works through the individual, and the mighty works of the Lord become apparent. You "will do even greater works than I have" (John 14:12).

In the Excarnational model the individual must leave behind his or her corrupt humanity to live in God. In the Incarnational model God joins us in our humanity. If the Lord finds us a suitable dwelling, why shouldn't we? Because we cannot find our own way to God, he will find his way to us.

Excarnational theology has influenced many movements throughout Christian history, and it has had an obvious effect on the lives of many famous Christians. Historically, it was used destructively by Manaches and Jansen and their followers; today it can be found somewhere within all Christian denominations, although it seems to be the most active among fundamentalists.

Incarnational theology was considered the main tradition in the early Christian communities, and it has remained the primary and formal teaching of the Catholic church (though, certainly, it was not always pastorally practiced) and also of several mainline Protestant churches. In the early church, St. John the Evangelist presents the Incarnational worldview.

Implications for Those Who Work in Ministry

Your own theology is not just a set of images through which you perceive yourself and God, and it is not just your perspective on other people. You will act on what you perceive; you will carry out what you know. So your ministerial style will be consistent with the way your beliefs are theologically encoded. This mind set will affect every aspect of ministry, daily tasks, worship, prayer, teaching, relationships, and professional style, and it will surface in the family, at school, in church, and in secular involvements.

Depending on your view of people (whether you believe they are basically good or basically evil), you will try to cooperate with God to save them, either by attempting to get God into their lives or call God out from within them. And because it doesn't seem to be possible to combine these two worldviews into one (we can't see ourselves as both basically good and basically evil simultaneously), there doesn't seem to be a way to reconcile the two approaches other than to say that God has a way to reach people who view things from both perspectives. In effect, God has something for everyone. Why not? It's just like God to do that!

Unfortunately, it's difficult to keep ministers in each theology from fighting each other. Their fighting not only confuses the people who are trying to listen to us, but it embarrasses us as credible announcers of the good news. Also it is plainly un-Christian.

There is one point of agreement that can help everyone work together. Both theologies stress the need for individual choice. To be saved, you have to choose God's love, you have to accept God's offer for a relationship. And at the end of the salvation process, both theologies acknowledge that God will work inside the individual.

But as each group tries to pinpoint how our relationship with God occurs and what its results are, there is bound to be the sound of theological gunfire as highly skilled and intelligent ministers of the gospel try to squeeze an unlimited being into limited images and categories. Wasn't it Voltaire who said: "God creted man in his own image and likeness, and man has been returning the compliment ever since"!

Although Excarnational and Incarnational might be convenient categories to help people clarify these two approaches, it would not be fair to suggest that everyone belonging to a certain church has automatically bought into the point of view that is stereotypically associated with that church. Few churches can claim that their congregations are made up of people who see things from only one of these perspectives. You can find Excarnational Catholics and Incarnational fundamentalists. You can find people who believe in the basic goodness of humanity worshiping alongside people who believe we are basically evil, whether it's in the mainline Protestant churches, evangelical communities, charismatic gatherings, conservative churchs, prayer groups, Bible study groups, or even clergy gatherings within the same denomination.

Your theological perspective doesn't really come just from your past training, or from parental images, community worship, the Christian ways of life you observe, or even from friends of various religious persuasions. All of these have made a contribution, but out of all those options and images available to you, you prefer one perspective or the other because it coordinates with your self-image.

These two theological perspectives, while they cannot be reconciled, give us a good picture of the way God works in scripture. God offers us a way to explain his activity in our lives whether we view ourselves and others as good or as evil. Anyone seeking God has a route available, and at the end of either process, if we accept the offer, we enjoy the love of God and are saved from loneliness, from permanent isolation, and from self-destruction.

Problems for Christians Working Together

Within church ministry teams, there will be some stress between people operating out of each theology as they try to work on ministerial tasks, because there won't be agreement on what the task is. Are we trying to convert people, educate them, or get them to go to church? Are we trying to make them feel their goodness or their corruptness? Do we want people to have information about God or to know God? Should we be praying more as a community or working more on ministry tasks?

As we assess our priorities, we will urge others to cooperate in our theological perspective. Excarnationalists will tend to be concerned with those not saved, emphasizing their evil nature and creating stress within families and between church members. They believe this is what God wants.

Incarnationalists, because they know people are basically good (even those people who don't know it yet), tend to be rather casual in proclaiming the good news, and may perhaps prefer to love everybody and let them figure it out for themselves. Even though God doesn't force a relationship, he doesn't ever stop presenting the options, so there needs to be some announcing and some teaching within the loving, too! Incarnationalists tend to be very quiet lovers. When the loving is accompanied by a clear reminder that this love we share is God, relationships become more than personal; they become apostolic.

It is easy to see why Excarnationalists and Incarnationalists often clash over worship. Because our worship expresses our theology, it makes our spiritual events visible. In the process what we believe and the way we believe it are expressed through images. Bcause all of the important images connect back to myself, I will want to celebrate and continue to experience God in ways I can recognize. If the images, signs, symbols, or expressions used in worship help me articulate my experience of God with the rest of the worshiping community, and also continue that experience, then I will participate actively. If this cannot happen, then I won't feel part of the worship.

Later we shall see that the main reason young people don't participate in Sunday liturgy is that the images used there don't connect with their own experience. And when they don't feel involved, they either attend the liturgies in a quiet rage or they vote with their feet: they leave, refusing to participate in something they don't understand. In the exceptional communities where youth enjoy worship, you can notice that the quality of their involvement is closely connected to their recognition of what is happening up in front as well as around them.

It is difficult to get Christians praying together when the people gathered together share differing theologies. When people of theology fail to find something they can recognize in public worship, they attack! And no one fights more intensely than religious people who view themselves as defending God and his revealed ways, when in fact they are probably only defending their own perspective on God. As Christian people, however, we must continue loving one another unconditionally and give up theological agreement as a condition for caring. Otherwise, we are going to see continued tension in worship, in classrooms, in homes, in staff meetings, in confirmation and first communion programs, and even in friendships.

If there is a place where people of both perspectives can meet and share, it is in the healing arena of unconditional love. We must meet at the heart, because we do not meet in mind. As I've pointed out, each group, each theology, is in touch with a different part of the elephant, which is the human condition. Somehow, through each theology, God ministers to the whole elephant. One group will continue to see mostly evil in the human condition and the other group will see mostly good. Why fight over which of two eyes sees better when you need both eyes to see in depth? "Don't judge your brother who has a stick in his eye when you have a board in your own eye. Remove the board in yours so you may better see a way to help your brother" (Matt. 7:3-5). We need both eyes!

If it takes two hands to clap, why is it that "the left hand doesn't know what the right hand is doing" (Matt. 6:3)? If it takes two ears to hear, why did St. Peter in defense of Jesus "cut off the ear" of a man involved in Jesus' arrest, only to have Jesus put it back on (John 18:10-11)? Apparently for reasons uncomfortable to us, but satisfactory to God, we will continue to be Church perceiving and ministering from both Excarnational as well as Incarnational viewpoints. Let's not fight. The elephant is waiting.

6. Incarnational Theology

By now, it should be clear that I find the Incarnational approach richer in content, wider in understanding, and essentially healthier from the standpoint of human growth than the Excarnational approach, although granting that many other people lead a delightful Christian life while operating in the other set of images.

For me, though, Incarnational theology offers great images to see God and other people, to understand Jesus, and to share myself in ministry. I appreciate better why I'm unhappy when I'm living out of relationships and why I'm happy, even though I'm stressed out at times, when I'm building and deepening my relationships, knowing that there is always more to discover, to unveil, in God, in others, and within myself. I live my life expecting to find good.

So I've written this book from my own perspective, and I am not alone in the way I see. The Catholic church claims this perspective as its primary model of understanding and proclamation. Like many Catholics, I wish that we would only live more fully what we say we believe. Other mainline churches also claim this perspective, and I must admit that I have enjoyed worshiping and studying with Incarnationally oriented Protestants much more than I have with Excarnationally oriented Catholics. But I still choose to live each day loving the people God sends along, no matter what their perspective.

I see Incarnational theology as a theology of relationships. The raw facts of human experience are that we have God the Father, God the Son, and God the Holy Spirit: three persons in God, three persons in perfect love, in perfect relationship. The God we worship is a community!

The community that we call God created us and invites us to experience this same sense of community, but it can't happen unless we agree to it. All of these facts flow together in a rich historical pattern that makes fascinating reading and good material for lively theological debate. Ultimately, this community is an invitation to friendship and teamwork and a relational journey during which we find in Jesus Christ that the God we thought was our distant destination is already dwelling within us. And through this Jesus we come to the Father, guided by the Holy Spirit.

As in all relationships, there is an occasional battle of wills, a struggle to keep loving someone who would rather be independent. But from beginning to end, salvation history is a story of relationships, some successful, some apparently not. In this story we see the clear intentions of God, we marvel at his commitment as he walks that tightrope of friendship, allowing us on one side to be free in our choices, but on the other side doing everything short of revoking our free will in order to stay in a friendship with us and keep us from destroying ourselves. How many friends do you have who work this hard to offer and keep a friendship?

Our salvation history begins, of course, in the beginning: God looks out into the chaos and creates. Not a bad model for those who work in the ministry: when you see chaos, do what God did—create! And everything God creates is good, and he recognizes this goodness as an extension of himself, of his very essence. So the core of our identity, and the core of the rest of creation, is goodness.

Why don't we believe this? I constantly meet people who tell me they're afraid to let me really know them, because when I see them as they are down deep, I won't like them. They have already come to think that their core is not good. And when other people say, "No matter how hard I try to be good, God still knows how bad I am," I hurt along with them, because they actually think that God sees them as evil to the core, when, in fact, that's only how they see themselves. We're good, and we get to spend our lifetimes finding this out.

At the peak of this creation pyramid comes man and woman, given the intelligence and free will to be caretakers of the earth. They share an intimacy with God, knowing goodness in person, and seeing his goodness reflected in one another and throughout creation. They realize that their free wills are a gift to them to use in ruling the earth, but, even more significant, to use in choosing whether they will be happy or unhappy. They have, in free will, the power to allow themselves to be loved and the power to love others. And the results of this choice will affect the way they take care of the earth. Unloved people tend to manipulate with their power; loved people tend to facilitate with their power.

Later, apparently with a single choice, man and woman say no to God, and no to the intimacy they had with God. And they receive just what they chose: independence from God, the loss of their face-to-face intimacy, and a new knowledge of evil. What you choose, you get. With choices come consequences; and a bad choice produces unpleasant consequences.

The consequence of their choice is that Adam and Eve now use the garden to hide from God. And although their nakedness hadn't been a problem earlier, because total exposure was part of their shared intimacy, now with the loss of intimacy, they find their nakedness inappropriate and embarrassing, and they cover themselves, veiling themselves from God and one another. From that point on in our salvation history, God appears veiled in images, such as the ark of the covenant and the law.

But all along God promises a redeemer, someone who will free us from the sin of Adam and Eve and restore us to the intimacy once enjoyed by Adam and Eve. He will invite us to remove the veil by revealing, removing his own veil, exposing his true identity: a clear invitation to intimacy.

This promise is fulfilled in the arrival of Jesus Christ, the God-Human, God in the flesh, God veiled by flesh from direct view. Later, at his death, he sheds his own body, his own veil of flesh, while we see the temple veil torn in two. At last, the fullness of revelation: God lives in humanity. We see in the Resurrection that we are the place where he lives, the temple of his power and presence. And wherever there is humanity, wherever there is flesh, Jesus will already be within the flesh, waiting to be unveiled.

As the message of Jesus unfolds, as we see him at work in the scriptures, and as we meet him daily in the flesh, we realize that neither the sin of Adam and Eve nor any sin we commit will ever prevent God from loving us. He has always loved us unconditionally, despite original sin. So our understanding of redemption cannot include the notion that Jesus had to appease an angry God and convince the Father to love us again.

Then what did happen? We saw earlier that because God has given men and women free will, and won't take this gift back, he has had to go along with the choices they have made, even if he has not liked those choices. If he reversed their choices or intercepted and nullified the consequences of those choices, then this gift of free will would only be a game, a pretense. But it isn't a game. Free will is real. The choices, good and bad, are real. And the consequences are real. God is good, and he loves us, but if we choose to destroy ourselves, he has to let us! He will protect us only from what is outside our control. What is within our control is up to us, both choices and consequences. And it can be scary to discover that God is serious about this!

Although God will not intercept or block the consequences of our choices, it is comforting to know that he will help us deal with them. But if we choose not to deal with the results of our choices, then he can't help us much. Many people I know want to be independent of God when they make their choices, but as soon as one of those choices produces bad results, they beg God to relieve them of the burden of their own choices! "Please, dear God, fill my head with all the knowledge I need to pass this test, because I didn't study last night!"

Sometimes we pray to God to cancel our own free will and make our choices for us. "Lord, make me love this person whom I really hate!" God must be answering, "Look, I'd be thrilled if you would love that person. I've been trying to help you do that. But I won't make you. But if you'll choose to love the person, I really will help you." Sometimes we work for God, and sometimes God works for us. If it's God's job, we work for him. If it's our job, like studying for a test, he works for us. He'll help us in our choices and help us deal with the results. But when the job is ours, he won't do the work for us. Otherwise he would be canceling our choices, and canceling the function of our free will.

Although God would not reverse the choice of the first man and first woman, he has offered to help us with the consequences. God has set up a situation where we can choose to be independent of him or choose the intimacy of a close friendship. Of course, it is still our choice, but the offer and the promise of friendship is there.

The Hebrew scriptures, sometimes called the Old Testament, help us see God throwing his whole kingdom into helping us deal with the decision of Adam and Eve to know evil. A covenant is offered by God, an agreement that God will not break even if we do. And as we know, we have broken our part of the agreement many times, but God has remained true to his word. In this covenant, God will be our God, and we will be his people (Jer. 31:1). He will call the few to be a sign to the many (Matt. 22:14), the rest of the world.

The more I grow in my own friendships and see myself restraining my urges to dictate the choices my friends should make, the more I appreciate the tremendous discipline God has in allowing us to make up our own minds. This is a discipline grounded securely in God's belief in us. Maybe this is something we need to know about God: free will means that he believes in us.

As salvation history brings us to the fulfillment of the promise, to the invitation brought personally by God to earth, we see the birth of Jesus, through the consent of Mary and Joseph. Jesus becomes the revelation of God's presence and power. His presence is now visible; his power will work through our humanity. Jesus is the word made flesh, the face we have been waiting for since the sin of Adam and Eve. Jesus is the solid image of God we can touch and see.

Through the Incarnation Jesus came to earth neither to cancel our free will nor to appease an angry Father in heaven. He is here to reveal how we can deal with the consequences of original sin. Jesus is here with a personal invitation to become friends with God, to rediscover and choose intimacy with God. He is here with an offer to remove the veil. If the veil between us and God is sin, he brings forgiveness to remove the guilt. If the veil is past hurts, he brings healing. If the veil is personal isolation, he is the way back to friendship. If the veil is confusion and ignorance, he is the truth we need. If the veil is the darkness of our own worthlessness, he is the light. Whatever we need, he has it. He offers it. He delivers it, personally.

And he stays with us. "I will be with you all days, even to the end of the world" (Matt. 28:20). This Incarnational event is permanent. He will live in our flesh, and we will be his body. We will be the ones who expose his presence and power within us. We will proclaim who is within us and between us.

It is exciting doctrine that the presence and power of God is revealed in the flesh by Jesus Christ, but practically speaking, we know it's God when we experience his unconditional love. And we won't be sure his love is unconditional until we make mistakes. Only when we experience the forgiveness of God will we know that god values us more than the sin. He wants to get rid of the mistake, not get rid of us. And forgiveness is the clearest form of unconditional love. We can see our mistakes as a sign of our own stupidity and worthlessness and end up in self-pity, worshiping the false god of shame at the altar of depression. Or we can bring our sins to the real God and experience his total love through forgiveness. No single act expresses God's unconditional love for us better than his forgiveness.

So the choice is now ours. Do we accept the invitation that God is offering us? And what are the good consequences we can expect from this choice? Of course we will see God's unconditional love at work in our life. And we know as we grow in the intimacy he offers us that he will never reject us. But what will this love do to us?

Healing and Renewal

Jesus has already revealed the many things we can expect love to do in us and through us, but two areas are important to mention: healing and renewal.

Healing the Hurts

Healing is a restoration to wholeness, a return to our original goodness and completeness. And so it is a sign of the power and presence of God. This is the work of Jesus: to reveal our real selves, our whole selves, along with the friendship of God. Friendship makes us more complete. Why shouldn't friends heal one another and return to wholeness?

And because all creation is good, the work of the demons is

to disguise this goodness, hide it from us, and deceive us into thinking all creation and all humanity is corrupt. Satan is hostile to creation because it is good. But Jesus comes to heal what is broken and make the world well again (Luke 7:22).

Also because most people think God is far too powerful to consider the ordinary concerns of the individual, Jesus spends a great deal of time with ordinary people, curing their ordinary hurts. This is part of the message: God cares about everyone, especially those who don't feel special.

We see Jesus, through his actions, as a person concerned about others. He doesn't preach a new political system. He doesn't present a full organizational model for the new church. He simply walks around talking to people. If they hurt, he heals them. If they are confused, he teaches them. If they are struggling with the law, he puts the law in its proper perspective. He is concerned about what they need.

Through Jesus we see the word of God in action. As St. James points out in his letter: "Faith without actions is dead" (James 2:26). In other words, if you love people, show them. Jesus is not just a preacher; he is the love he preaches. He usually avoids the spectacular miracles because he is not a showman; he is God living in humanity and deeply concerned about people.

The miracles of Jesus are a tangible and visible sign of the presence of God and the power of the kingdom. They force people to confront a new experience and ask questions, and his healings shake their images of God as well as their set perceptions of the way the world works. The miracles of Jesus rattle people's worldviews.

These healings also *demand* faith, at least the faith of the person being cured. Someone has to believe in someone else outside of his or her control. A relationship! When I've exhausted every option I know, there are still plenty of options for God. Why not ask? But these feelings also *strengthen* faith. For those who have come to expect the unexpected from God, their faith will be rewarded. If you have spent your life living in an intimate relationship with God, you just know that the Lord loves to do the extra things we need. He loves it when we run out of wine! Or bread! Or doctors! Miracles show us a God who just loves to be needed.

And yet Jesus knows there is more to a person than bread and wine or healthy limbs. He even knows there is more to life than this life. Certainly Jesus healed many people of physical ailments, but the good experience lasted only a short time. So now they could walk or see. But were they happy? Would a physical cure make them happy?

Jesus reveals two major themes through his healing. Of course, these cures substantiated Jesus' claim to divinity. And they also underlined his concern for the spiritual life of the individual involved. But there is something in each cure for all of us. As Jesus cures an individual, he is also talking to all of us. As he works on a physical problem, we can also see him addressing a spiritual problem and its solution.

We need to look to the spiritual value of these miracles to see the proclamation Jesus intends for us all to hear. It would be easy to dismiss any of the miracles, figuring they don't apply to us because "I don't have that problem." But when we look again and see the spiritual equivalent of these miracles, we can all say, "There I am!"

Let's look at some of the major cures of Jesus and see what some of the spiritual messages might be:

THE BLIND MAN   *Matt. 9:27–31 and 20:29–34; Mark 8:22–26 and 10:46–52; Luke 18:39–43; John 9:1–41*

How many blind men did Jesus cure in the Gospel? It seems he was constantly curing someone who couldn't see. Isn't blindness, in fact, a perception problem? An imaging problem? Doesn't it mean that we can't see what is before us? And isn't that also a faith problem: seeing God? Seeing the one hidden, veiled from our view? All of these questions reveal the spiritual equivalent of blindness: the inability to see what's really out there. And most of us need more than one touch to be healed!

THE DEAF MUTE   *Mark 7:32–37*

In this story we have a man who can't hear or speak. Spiritually, he has lost the ability to hear or speak to God, to others, or even himself. Is our problem that we can't hear? Or won't listen? Is it that we can't speak about what is really important? Or won't share our feelings and experiences? Maybe we aren't ready to expose our real selves to others. In any case, if we can't or won't conduct a dialogue, we need to be healed.

THE LEPER *Mark 1:40–42*

Leprosy is a physical disorder that causes the deterioration of the skin and serious disfiguring. In the biblical story, as this disease progressed, it turned the individual's skin into a collection of open sores, rendering the person ugly and offensive to healthy people. Spiritually, do we think we're ugly, evil, corrupt? And what if this perception of ourselves keeps us from knowing the good and beautiful self created by God? Do we let others around us convince us that we're ugly? Does our sense of ugliness keep us from life-giving relationships? Do we point to places in our spiritual or physical features that have deteriorated? Or can we see our wholeness, and use that strength to reverse any deterioration? Whether the problem is physical or spiritual ugliness, Jesus is interested in our health, and our happiness.

THE PARALYTIC *Mark 2:1–12*

Paralysis means the loss of mobility in part of the body. Spiritually, paralysis means the loss of the ability to grow in relationships with God, or with other people, and possibly even with one's self. When you're not moving spiritually, you're paralyzed, frozen in your growth. Usually fear plays a major role in bringing us to a halt in our spiritual journey, leaving us afraid to ask for help, afraid to continue friendships, afraid to talk to God, and afraid to take risks. In the Gospel story of the cure of the paralyzed man, four friends played a significant role in getting him in touch with Jesus and tearing off the roof in order to lower him on his pallet to the feet of Jesus. Jesus linked his problem to forgiveness. Doesn't forgiveness free us to move again and continue our relational journey, letting us experience the unconditional love that heals our fear of being rejected?

MARY MAGDALENE *Luke 8:2*

Obviously a lot of us are spiritual law breakers. And yet, even breaking the law can be forgiven. Jesus knows that guilt can be removed, and he wants to find the way to help. Unloading guilt is a big step in getting a relationship going again.

THE CENTURION'S SERVANT   *Matt. 8:5–10; Luke 7:1–10*

In this miracle Jesus is not just strengthening the faith of believers in formal religion. He is using the faith of a "nonmember," showing us that personal faith is acceptable for healing. It may also remind us that we need to heal the problems we have with people of different religions.

LAZARUS   *John 11:1–44*

We can be sure that raising Lazarus from the dead was a great exercise of Jesus' power, and it certainly was a mark of his caring for Lazarus. It also spoke volumes about Jesus' power over death. But we should note that Lazarus did die again a few years later. No doubt Lazarus' resurrection was awe-inspiring to those who witnessed it, and Lazarus' family must have been stunned and delighted. But the Gospel presents this story for us so that its spiritual value is not lost. Jesus can bring us back from anything that buries us, anything that takes the life out of us. If we are spiritually dead, even rotting, Jesus can call us back to life if we allow it. It is to be hoped that our relationships are dying and rising to new life every day.

In any event, Jesus uses his healing power not only out of care for the individual, but also as a proclamation for others, reminding all of us that the spiritual healings are greater than the physical ones. But the physical ones are so delightfully tangible, so measurable, so earthy. They are great events in themselves.

Renewal: Healing the Scars

Just as healing is the process of curing our hurts, restoring us to our original wholeness, renewal is the ongoing process of returning us to the way we were when we were part of newly created humanity. *Healing* helps us deal with the hurts; *renewal* helps us deal with the scars caused by the hurts, the damage left behind by the hurt.

As he heals us, Jesus is not only concerned that we rediscover our original goodness but he wants us to live like new, free not only of any hurt but of the fear of being hurt. Just because you are no longer paralyzed or blind doesn't mean that you won't live in the terror of returning to that condition. So Jesus is also interested in the fears and anxieties that may cause you to hesitate to enter relationships, where you could be hurt again.

The goal of renewal is to give us the confidence to enter any dangerous situation, trusting in the power and presence of God. And because ministry is the area of relationships and relationships can produce plenty of hurt, we need the gift of boldness or confidence to allow us to return to the scene of previous hurt and know that our fear of being hurt will never stop us from dealing effectively with our relationships.

If ministry is caring for people in relationships, then Jesus doesn't want us cowering in the face of a relationship. His love offers us the chance to be renewed, brought back to the boldness and confidence of Adam and Eve before they sinned. And if we can experience in ourselves that the power of God can heal any hurt, and even reduce our fear of being hurt, then we know that we will always be able to count on that power in the future, releasing any barriers to loving that we might experience. That is confidence. And that is what Jesus guarantees.

With his presence, Jesus is saying "I am with you everyday" (Matt. 28:20). With his power he is saying "You can do even greater things than I have." But for the sake of the integrity of his relationship with us, and out of deep respect for us, he must wait until we choose to allow this power and presence to change us, and then through us, to change others.

Fear: The Enemy of Relationships

What will keep us from making the choice to allow Jesus to change us is, more than anything else, fear. Because of previous hurts, some healed, some not yet healed, we are afraid to begin again, begin anew. We are actually afraid of being renewed.

Our fear of renewal can make us, like Adam and Eve, hide, keeping us veiled within existing relationships so we don't grow. Or fear can make us hide from relationships so we can never be hurt again. Either way, fear can keep us from knowing someone deeply and being known; and, consequently, can keep us from loving someone deeply and being loved. And if fear is that powerful in preventing us from being renewed, then this is something that personally concerns the Lord.

Another way to look at it is that fear makes us hesitate to make choices. It stands in the way of our using our free will effectively, distorting our options and terrorizing us with old feelings of hurt. Fear can even be the reason so many people numb themselves to any feelings at all.

When we numb ourselves to our own feelings so that we don't have to relive the bad memories, we end up numbing one of the ways we perceive life within us and around us. And numbing our perceptions reduces our ability to choose. People use many devices to numb themselves: drugs, alcohol, fantasy, even religious activity. But in any case, repressing our fears and numbing ourselves will always diminish our power to choose. And when you cannot choose effectively, you are messing with your power to love and be loved. How can you love without choosing? How can you be happy when all of your routes to discovering this happiness are closed by fear?

So fear can make us hide ourselves inside our relationships, and it can keep us from ever beginning good relationships. Ultimately, it can conceal our free will from us and keep us from making life-giving choices or ruining the few good relationships we have.

If you fear being hurt, you will never expose yourself, and therefore never love deeply. You need the confidence that renewal can offer. If you strongly fear being hurt, even if your hurt has already been healed, you will never act boldly to make the decisions to begin or maintain healthy relationships. You need more than healing. You need renewal, a return to the confidence and boldness that man and woman had when they were new, acting clearly out of their basic goodness.

Fear also hurts our relationships by causing us to lose confidence in others' ability to choose. So we manipulate them to make what we consider to be the right choices. We play with their feelings instead of respecting their free will because, we say, "I don't want them to be hurt as I have been hurt." That's a lofty motive, but not the way God works. When we manipulate others we have more people living in fear, more people terrorized by their feelings, and we are a contributor to that fear! Helping them? Hardly. We're destroying them!

By manipulating someone to accept options we consider valuable, but not really letting them choose freely, they will never really own their choice, and when we're not around later, they won't act out that choice as their own. Manipulation doesn't help anyone. It tells the person we're manipulating that "I really don't believe you can manage your life yourself." And it also is a confession on our part, "I don't want to go through the process of helping you look at all the options, especially the really bad ones. I don't want to go through the hassle and agony of waiting for you to make the right choice." And it finally says, "I don't want to allow you any bad consequences, because I can't handle it! I don't want you to hurt so I don't have to hurt!"

Because fear makes us hide and makes us manipulate, it keeps us from allowing God to work freely in our lives while still leaving us free to choose. God certainly knows that if people don't accept his guidance, if they don't see from his message which options are life-giving and which ones aren't, then facing the consequences of their choices will teach them to make better decisions next time. But people don't always face the consequences. More than likely, people remain immature because they never deal honestly with the consequences of their choices. If I make a bad decision, and I either block out the consequences or someone helps me avoid them, then I don't feel or see the bad effect, so it doesn't seem like a bad choice. Maybe I can get away with doing the same thing again! The better road to maturity is to allow the consequences to hit me squarely, to feel and see the results of my choice, and conclude that this is not a good choice for next time.

I can help struggling persons like this in two ways: I can guide them in reviewing their options, leaving them free to choose for themselves; and I can help them deal honestly and effectively with the consequences of their final choice without intercepting the consequences so they don't have to deal with them. But if I am overcome by my own fear of hurting along with them, then I won't be much of a friend. I certainly won't help them. And I'll really be telling them that "I don't think you can make your own free choices, so let me make them for you, or at least let me help you avoid the consequences, so I don't hurt with you while you deal with the consequences."

This kind of manipulation occurs frequently in friendships and in families, but we also dictate others choices in the name of religion. Teaching that presents and helps people review their options is one thing. But once we start enforcing an option because it's the right one, then we are manipulating. Many times in the Gospels we can see Jesus teaching, presenting the kingdom, showing us the best options for growth, but never making people choose an option they aren't willing to make their own. Religion should get out of the enforcement business.

Teaching can also play an effective role in helping people deal with the consequences of what they do. A good teacher can facilitate a tremendous change in a person's life at a moment of crisis, as long as there is no manipulation. Unfortunately, well-meaning people are the best manipulators if they haven't dealt effectively with their own fears. Find the manipulators in society, and you will find fear at work.

Instead Jesus shows us another way: his invitation is to move away from the kingdom of fear and become part of his kingdom of love, where free choices are always honored. If our religious programs intensify people's guilt instead of helping them relieve it, then we are preaching the wrong kingdom. If our programs scare people into operating according to certain behavior codes, even if the behavior is called Christian, instead of teaching them how to choose freely, then we are teaching the wrong kingdom. And if we imply that the good new is that "You're a bad person; you're a sinner, and only the law can save you, so do what you're told!" then we're not proclaiming the good news at all! Jesus is a God who trusts us, believes in us, and reveals to us that we are good, that we can be happy, that our relationships can work, and that we are free to choose. He will teach us the best options, but no matter what we choose, he will help us deal with the consequences, never withdrawing his presence, always offering his power that forgives us when our choices are bad, heals us when our choices hurt, and renews us when our hurts leave scars.

Jesus knows that if he can encourage even a few people to live this way, then they can proclaim his kingdom in confidence. He is embarrassed by people in the church who offer a kingdom of enforcement, of manipulation, of guilt. That is exactly the kingdom that he came to free us from! Is it any wonder that the people who make Jesus so angry in the Gospels are the Pharisees? This was the kingdom they ran, "laying burdens on people in the name of God, burdens impossible to carry" (Matt. 23:4).

What changes the church is what changes the disciples, and what changes society is what changes the church: the unconditional love of God, his real power, and his guarantee to remain with us and in us, which is his presence. If we can allow ourselves to accept his invitation to a relationship, then we will be changed, our guilt no longer feeding our fears, our past hurts no longer manipulating us into manipulating others. We will be renewed, confident, bold, knowing that if it works for us, it can work for others. We can preach, announce, and proclaim the kingdom of Jesus Christ because we are part of that kingdom, we are disciples changed by his love, and as changed people we can change the church. And a renewed church can change society, or at least issue a clearer, more personal invitation to change. Nothing is automatic. None of this is easy. But what would you rather do with the rest of your life?

If guilt can be forgiven, and hurts can be healed, and even the scars left over after healing can be removed so that we are like new, renewed, then "what can keep us from the Love of God?" (Rom. 8:35). What can keep us from building and maintaining good relationships with God, others, and ourselves? What can keep us from getting involved in other people's lives?

If Jesus can leave a safe heaven and come to earth to be incarnate in our lives, becoming part of our experience, then why can't we leave our safe churches, our secure homes, and enter into the experience of others?

If Jesus himself grew and struggled with his relationships, then we who follow him, we who are his disciples, cannot expect to avoid the same struggles. And we certainly cannot expect him to do this for us. But with us—yes. Jesus does not replace us so we don't have to relate to anyone or make any decisions. Instead he goes with us to others, and also waits for our arrival already within them. Even in relationships he is the beginning and the end, the alpha and the omega! He is the way to love, the truth we discover, and the life we live—all in relationships!

If the kingdom of God's power and incarnate presence is in fact to be found in the everyday world of relationships, then the kingdom of evil and destruction that can ruin our relationships is fear. We must learn to confront and choose against this evil force, which hides our goodness and obscures our vision of reality.

In my own ministry, and in working with ministers trying to live in God's love and share it daily, I have seen what fear can do. I have witnessed its arrival and departure in people's lives, I have seen it dominate and destroy, and I have seen it conquered. I have known it to disappear, and then come back. I have seen many of its disguises and veils. It can attract and repel, make you take shortcuts, or not try at all. It can be a brick wall that will knock you silly when you run into it, or it can be a mirage that looks like a brick wall so you won't run in that direction.

Sometimes the only way to tell a real brick wall from a mirage is to run at it, knowing that if it's real and you are hurt crashing into it, you can claim the gift of healing from God. If it's not real, you have run through the veil of bricks and discovered a new way to grow, just what the mirage was trying to hide. I've often uttered the phrase that is familiar to my friends and probably characteristic of my ministry style: "Onward, into the brick wall!"

I know at times I can seem foolish, and at other times wise. But wisdom usually comes from being a bit foolish and then learning from the experience. There is an old saying "Good judgment comes from experience, experience comes from bad judgment." In steering you toward confronting your fears, I know I'm asking you to run at a lot of brick walls. Some will hurt you, and some will be only mirages that will part like a veil to reveal new routes to incredible journeys. But you can recover from being hurt: the Lord guarantees that. You can't recover from standing still, staying safe and uninvolved. You cannot bury your gift in the ground; the one Jesus praises is the person who risks all gifts and thus multiplies them (Matt. 25:24–30).

Likewise, we have two sacraments for those who are hurt in relationships, who are damaged while running at brick walls. We have the sacrament of reconciliation, if your spirit is hurt, and the sacrament of anointing of the sick, if your body is hurt. We have no sacrament for someone who doesn't try.

Fear will make you not want to try. I know; I've been there. I'm still there sometimes. Perhaps I can at least clarify some of the areas where fear does its best work, so you can review your options. I can't make your choices, and you can't make mine, but I can certify that you can survive your fears. I am surviving mine.

Fear can completely hide your goodness, if you give it permission. It runs a kingdom all its own, using suspicion and feelings of regret or worthlessness to make you believe you are someone other than the person God created. Fear supplies you with a false identity. It is a kingdom of deceit.

Fear will always be there, but it cannot run your life or make your decisions unless you let it. As with all feelings, either you own fear, or fear owns you. If you allow it to make your decisions, it will ruin you. But if you can take charge of it, using the power of Jesus within you, and certain of your own basic goodness as you choose, then the kingdom of fear cannot rule you. You rule it!

To which kingdom do you want to belong? To which one will you choose to belong? Which one will present and review your options, which one will be your friend, no matter what the consequences? You cannot destroy either God or fear, but you can decide for whom you want to work, and you can choose which one you want to work for you.

Four Fears That Cripple

In my own experience in ministry and in my contact with other ministers, I have come to see the many ways fear can thwart real growth. Fear has become an enemy I respect deeply enough to stay alert to its many disguises, a force in our lives that will always present its destructive options whenever choices are to be made.

Although fear can take many forms, four types play a prominent role in destroying us, or at least in veiling our goodness. I am talking about the fear of failure, the fear of rejection, the fear of pain, and the fear of death.

Fear of Failure

Our society places great emphasis on the earning ethic; in some form, we are constantly being told that we *are* what we *do*. Each person is expected to work to become something—a teacher, a scientist, an athlete, whatever—and the greatest American insult is to call someone lazy. Failure to achieve means you have no worth, no value as a person. Because you haven't earned your worth, you can't really be someone.

Watch the way people introduce themselves to one another. As soon as names are exchanged, the next question is "And what do you do?" This is a way we have of measuring each other. Because the spiritual part of a person is so hard to define, we have settled for something easier to measure: roles and tasks.

Is it any wonder, then, that we live in the constant fear of failure? In a society where doing is being, then failure to do is really a failure in being a person. So some of us keep taking on more tasks because we have this tremendous need to do things. At the same time we have a deep fear of failing at any of these tasks, so even if we're not doing them very well, we must maintain the appearance that we are successful, even if we have to lie, cheat, or steal in order to keep up that image. Our children have learned these lessons well in school, in sports, in shopping, and we will see them later applying what they've learned in business and in relationships.

Others of us do just the opposite: we won't try anything because we might fail. We are always hesitant, we never take risks, and we are full of reasons why a project or an idea will never work.

Spiritually, Jesus challenges us to take our worth from him. Although there are certainly some tasks in his kingdom, carrying out these duties expresses our worth; it does not earn it. Our worth is already given to us: we are "worth more than many sparrows" (Matt. 10:31) to our Father. He doesn't expect us to earn that worth. So in reality, our worth is already within us, and our actions will express this worth in the way we treat other people and go about our worldly tasks. Who needs to earn anything? It's all free!

What a challenging message for those of us who try to over-achieve by taking on too many tasks in order to prove our worth. What a statement for those of us who won't do anything out of fear that a failure will announce our worthlessness.

Our tasks can help us find out what our talents are and what they're not. So failure, if we've put forth our best effort, can tell us where we aren't gifted, and help bring us to an honest awareness of our limitations. And if we haven't tried hard enough, failure can challenge us to a better effort next time.

Failure, in fact, can be a form of revelation; if we learn from failures instead of dodging them, we can grow in our apprecia-tion of ourselves. And because there will always be plenty of failures to learn from, we can approach our daily tasks confi-dent that if we do our best in the work we have, we will be ex-pressing our faith in God and announcing God's faith in us. If we fail in some of these tasks, it's no judgment on our worth as a person. We can either find out we should work harder, or dis-cover that the task isn't ours to do. Either way, we've learned something. We will fail occasionally, but we don't have to go through life so terrified of failure that we either take on too much or do too little.

I remember meeting a little kid who had just been asked by an adult what he wanted to be when he grew up. He said, "Happy." This little guy already had the wisdom of the saints. I hope the world doesn't retrain him.

If we deal effectively with the fear of failure, we can spend the rest of our days being valuable people in love, and our tasks will proclaim that this love is now our power, and the Lord's presence certifies our worth. We will no longer feel we must earn our salvation; we will only feel the need to an-nounce it!

The feeling of fear is something you will probably always carry with you, and this feeling will vary in intensity; you will probably never eliminate fear completely. Just remember: feelings don't have any morality. The moral issues don't start until you begin to act on your feelings. So if you allow fear to run your life, you've made a choice, and there will be damaging consequences.

The moral (and therefore, life-giving) task of Christians is to listen to all our feelings, and then select the best available option. As a rule, feelings aren't very good decision-makers, and, in this case, fear will destroy you if it is allowed to make your decisions.

The best way to take charge of the fear of failure is to identify it clearly when it shows up in your consciousness. Get it out there on the table. Then you can see it as one of your options, but certainly not a force controlling your life. Many people have been trained to suppress feelings, especially negative ones. This gives you the illusion that you've gotten rid of the feeling, when in fact you've only hidden it, pushed it under the table where it will roam around until it shows up somewhere else in your psyche, usually as a form of neurosis.

In therapy a person with a controlling fear is brought back to a major experience that generated the fear and is given a new opportunity to deal effectively with that feeling. Therapy identifies what fear owns you and offers you the chance to take ownership over it. Suppose you had a bad experience in childhood, and you buried the fear that was created by the event. In therapy you can put the experience and the feeling on the table, and will, it is hoped, understand the experience enough to select a healthier response, freeing yourself from the old fear. So the goal of therapy is to hand you back to yourself. Usually God will take this opportunity to invite you to reorganize your life a little bit, orienting your choices into healthier patterns and developing better images of yourself and others.

Although professional therapists are helpful when fear severely dominates a person's life, most therapy occurs when two friends are honest with one another in an atmosphere of trust. Prayer can be therapeutic too, especially if God is allowed to have the chance to talk. These moments can seem painful, but God is simply doing what a good friend will always do: calling you to confront areas in you life that keep you from growing and being happy.

The fear of failure is usually developed in childhood. Through a series of events a child learns that his or her self-worth is connected to successful achievement. This message is reinforced in many ways. Parents who are success-oriented need to have successful children who compete well in academics and athletics. So they send out a Don't Fail message. Coaches who fear failing send out a Don't Fail message. It doesn't take a child long to figure out what to do to keep adults happy: succeed.

So tasks become an endless series of showdowns, where I have to prove myself again and again. If this attitude is carried into adult roles, then these roles become tools to earn my self-worth. I have to be a successful parent or priest or nun to feel OK. And I expect the people around me to help me feel I'm doing well in my role. Beware! Roles can be veils if they hide me from myself, others, and God.

All of this is motivated by my fear of failure. I must not look stupid. If I am a youth minister I won't delegate responsibility to the young people around me, because they might fail, and that would reflect poorly on me. If I am a pastor I won't share my duties with laypeople because it would look as though I was not doing my job. If I am a parent I will send my teenager to confirmation classes whether or not he or she wants to go, because I need to feel I'm doing my parental duty.

I'm not saying that we shouldn't carry out our proper roles in a responsible way. But it is irresponsible and destructive to use roles *just* to make ourselves feel OK. If I use a role just to feel powerful, or just to get recognition, or just to have an identity or value, then I am probably motivated by the fear of failure, the fear that leads me to think that being something means being someone.

This fear can control everything from our choice of clothes to our choice of social companions. It can make us procrastinate, put off things when we might fail. It can generate panic over school examinations. This fear is even at the root of some anxiety-linked learning dysfunctions.

Some people are so certain they will fail at anything that failure is the only thing they can do successfully! I've seen people who thrive on it! They milk their failures to draw attention to themselves. Just watch people who love to moan about how badly everything is going for them.

Many husbands and wives who are having problems in their marriage or parents who are having difficulties with their children won't go for counseling because it means admitting failure. The same is true of alcoholics and workaholics.

Jesus Christ attacks our fear of failure by first reminding us of our worth and then turning his kingdom over to us. He's saying "I believe in you!" God believes in us more than we do. God shares his power with us, but we are afraid we might fail. We bury our talents, our worth, in the ground, and then we go out and try to earn our worth through our own efforts. We have become suspicious of a gift, and we trust only what we earn. How American!

In the face of all of this, the Lord of time spends his time waiting, inviting, revealing another way to live. There is life beyond fear. There is success even in failure at times. But there is no success in fear. There is no personal worth that hasn't already been given to us.

If it weren't so sad, it would be comical to watch the sexual-stereotype struggle. I need to feel male, so I use my male equipment: macho! I need to feel feminine, so I use my female equipment: alluring! How shall we spend our time together? Let's have sex. Even sex has become a way of reducing male and female roles to a task. "Please, tell me I was good!"

Fear of Rejection

The next fear involves failure in a relationship with another person. The fear of rejection means that we are terrified that when we offer ourselves in a relationship, we will be turned down, avoided, or even ignored. And this will confirm that there is someting wrong with us as persons.

This fear can occur at the initiation of a relationship when we say in some way, "Hi, want to be friends?" and the response, either real or imagined, is "No!" So we feel rejected.

Or this fear may surface after we have begun a relationship and want to move from casual contact into a deeper friendship. Our fear will keep us from asking for more depth, so we stay stuck at the existing and superficial level of communication.

The fear of rejection will not allow us to pursue a relationship to any depth because we are fearful that something in us may be discovered that will make the other person bail out. So we wear masks and try to be whatever the other person will accept. This fear betrays the fact that we don't feel good about ourselves, and we know the other person will find that out if we get any deeper.

The fear of rejection keeps us from telling friends something they don't want to hear, even if it is something they need to hear. So the honesty level is compromised, and the real feelings and difficulties we have are never shared. As a result, we'll never really know one another, and we'll never be able to depend on our friendships.

So our relationships are just arrangements in which we agree to spend some time together as long as nothing surfaces that will be too serious or difficult to deal with. This is the fear that runs a peer group, affecting not only young people, but even adults.

This is the fear that fosters conditional acceptance: "You can come along with us if you wear what we wear, if you listen to our music, if you talk our slang, if you hang around the people we like." The fear of rejection drives us into if-groups and into if-partnerships because we are sure no one will accept us unconditionally. And because we believe that conditional acceptance is the only thing possible in the real world, then we accommodate ourselves to reality and negotiate relationships that demand some ifs with which we can live.

This pattern is easy to see in adolescents who belong to a school culture featuring a constant process of negotiation for a place to belong, a gang with which to run, a group in which to feel safe. Almost nowhere in the adolescent world can genuine unconditional love be found. An individual's need to belong somewhere combines with the fear of rejection to produce a young person who will settle for conditional acceptance rather than be left alone. If we can't find unconditional love, the only option is to join a group or find a friend who will tolerate us, and maybe even enjoy us—as long as we follow the norms of the unwritten contract.

Peer groups obviously have these contracts, but dating also

involves these pressures. If you love me, you will (fill in the blank). And of course an insecure person, fearing rejection, will conform! What young person, already feeling isolated from adults, wants to be isolated also by peers?

I call this phenomenon a peer trap because, to the young person, there doesn't seem to be a way out of this condition. But young people aren't the only ones affected by this fear of rejection. Adults carry this fear from their own adolescence into their marriages, social groups, occupations, and even religious practices. When adults find themselves saying "My spouse will love me if _____; my friends will appreciate me if _____; my boss will like me if _____; God will love me if _____," then they are operating under the control of the fear of rejection.

So adults, raised in the syndrome of conditional acceptance generated by this culturally imbedded fear, also suffer from the same patterns as young people, only in subtler forms. The pressure that runs country clubs, taverns, offices, singles groups, neighborhoods, and even families sometimes is the fear of rejection, motivating people to settle for conditional acceptance (the big If) rather than face no acceptance.

Only God offers this incredible unconditional love, which is the manifestation through us of God's power and presence. In the early days of the church, pagans who couldn't discern the full revelation of the risen Christ certainly knew love when they saw it. "See how these Christians love one another!" The church today, invested with his power and presence, is in a unique position to proclaim God's unconditional love by loving people unconditionally and telling them why. "Even if a mother should reject her child, I will not reject you" (Ps. 27:10).

So if a church community proclaims by its behavior that "God will love you if _____," then that group is not faithful to its mandate to preach the truth. If a prayer group can pray only with people who gain their approval, then they must be praying to the false god If. If church communities cannot proclaim God's unconditional love in this world, then we have abandoned our mission and become just another institution veiling the truth, hiding from humanity the good news of the power and presence of Christ, and leaving the world to grope for some meaning in relationships scarred by conditional acceptance.

Although there is no if on the part of God when giving unconditional love, we know that each person must, in some way, agree to be loved. This acceptance of God's love is salvation from isolation and loneliness. This unconditional love is the only thing that offers a person a way out of the peer trap.

As church, then, we have a great opportunity to offer the world just what it needs. We have a message that will be good news to those who have given up hope that unconditional love is even possible. But if we don't proclaim and live this good news ourselves in our relationships, then who needs us? Who needs one more if-group? Who needs another if-partner? As church, we have the chance to give people exactly what they need. But we can't give what we don't have ourselves. So we come back to dealing wiith the fear that hides God's love from us: the fear of rejection.

If we are dominated by this fear, we don't believe we are already loved totally by God. We don't need to search for other forms of acceptance once we've experienced and agreed to God's unconditional love. "If God is for us, who can be against us?" (Rom. 8:31).

So your fear quotient is a pretty good indicator of your faith in God. If you're still wondering what others will think of you or trying to gain their acceptance, or keeping up with the Joneses, then you still aren't fully renewed in Christ. The fear of rejection is still partially running your life.

Once you allow the Lord to be fully what he wants to be within you, you will live in the certainty of being loved. You will avoid the disguises of arrogance, and live, instead, in the humble confidence of your own worth. And if someone can't love you and accept you as you are, that's that person's problem!

My favorite image of the Christian who has a good faith-relationship with God is of a person who, having overcome his or her fear of rejection, can walk up to a stranger and say sincerely, "Hi! You're gonna like me!" Now I call that faith! If you are honestly loved and are confident in that love, even though you may have many faults, then why not let what's good about you help overcome what isn't? Why not live in the confidence that God's love is stronger than your faults?

This confidence doesn't mean we can sit back and bask in God's love and let the rest of the world continue its lonely search. Quite the opposite. No one receives good news without sharing it! Who would "put their lamp under a bushel basket" (Matt. 5:15)? If we are to help people who still live their lives governed by the fear of rejection, we must stay in relationships with them and model how we make our own choices without being dominated by this fear. We can also help others by helping them identify their fear of being rejected and allowing them to talk it out in the security of our acceptance of *them*, which is not the same as acceptance of their behavior. If God waited until he approved of our behavior before he accepted us, then he would never accept us! We must try to love others the same way.

Doing so means loving with the eyes of God, not with the eyes of the world. The world sees faults, and so does God, but God also sees the person's true worth. And we need this vision to stay fixed on the real person, while that same person, no doubt, will test us severely with his or her behavior. If you think that's frustrating to you, then think how frustrating that is for God!

Remember, these people have been told for years that they're no good, and they're acting that way because they believe that about themselves. Who is going to show them anything else? Who is going to show them their real selves? Who is going to invite them to like themselves?

And do you expect them to awaken to this new discovery without a fight? Change is frightening: don't you think they will struggle to preserve their old familiar identity, while you wrestle with them to convince them of their beauty?

If you intend to love as God does, then plan on being frustrated, as God is. Imagine! In the name of religion, people have been told that they're no good. And many religious leaders actually consider this to be their mission. No wonder Jesus vented his anger on the Scribes and Pharisees! (This insight has worked wonders in taming my own clerical righteousness.)

It's difficult to convince people to believe that they're lovable and acceptable. It is easier to get people to believe that they're no good, and therefore bound to be rejected by God and by others. The fear of rejection comes equipped with all the excuses that explain why relationships cannot work. The fear of rejection gives us the certitude that we can never be in a satisfying relationship with anyone, especially God. And because love can only be experienced in a relationship, this fear, if allowed to dominate us, will keep us from being fully loved.

On the other hand, once we allow ourselves to be loved completely by God, that will cancel all the excuses we've been using to avoid building effective relationships. I love the story about Peter and John going up to the temple to pray and coming across a lame man who is begging at the Beautiful Gate. His condition is his excuse for begging, and he asks Peter and John for a donation. But, like all ministers I know, they're broke. Peter has another currency, though, and offers it: "I don't have silver or gold, but what I have I'll give you. In the name of Jesus Christ, get up and walk" (Acts 3:6). The man gets up, walks, and then jumps around. The good news is he's cured. The story doesn't mention a later realization, which must have hit him like a ton of bricks: "I'm cured. But now I don't have an excuse to beg. My career as a beggar is ended. I have to get a real job!"

God delights in curing us and taking away our excuses. He loves to help us deal with our fear of rejection because we use that fear so effectively to stay out of relationships. If he can help us remove the fear as a dominating force in our lives, then he knows we have a much better chance of living our lives responsibly, seeing and enjoying his power and presence, and helping reveal this good news to others.

Fear of Pain

We all carry a fear of pain in our bodies that motivates us to avoid physical injury. That fear is a healthy fear. The damaging fear of pain is the strong fear of relational pain: the unwillingness to deal with the hurts that accompany relationships, especially relationships of depth.

Although the fears of failure and rejection usually occur early in a relationship, the fear of pain surfaces and is sharply felt after a relationship has been going for a while. Just when you believe you have dealt effectively enough with the first two fears and have finally allowed yourself to pursue relationships as a part of your spirituality, then you will find the fear of pain waiting to be addressed. The fear of rejection makes you afraid of *getting* close to someone; the fear of pain makes you afraid of *staying* close to someone.

The fear of pain shows up in the deeper relationship struggles with the people to whom we are already committed: spouse, good friends, ministry teammates, parents, children. This fear makes us intolerant of their annoying habits or mannerisms and resentful about spending extra time with them, hurting with them, struggling to be sensitive to them, dealing with their moods and unique qualities, and, especially, waiting for them to grow.

The struggle of staying with people we love seems to take up an enormous amount of time, and it involves plenty of pain. You have a child and she demands a lot of your attention, and you wonder if it's all worth it. You married someone twenty years ago and last year he became crippled for life. He now requires a deeper level of your commitment, reminding you that you promised to love him for better or for worse. And you wonder if you can endure it. You have a friend who has always been available, but suddenly is dealing with a personal crisis. This time your friend needs you, and you find yourself counting the cost of friendship. The fear of pain will invite you to bail out of the effort, and even bail out of the relationship. It hurts too much to love deeply and unconditionally. This is usually the fear that terminates marriages: the fear of pain, the feeling that it is too much trouble. This is the fear that ends friendships: "It was too painful; I couldn't take it anymore."

The fear of pain, if we give in to it, will prevent us from waiting for someone else to grow. It tempts us to jump in and try to force a person to grow in the way we want and when we want. We just don't want to struggle with the relationship any longer.

But what couple ever grows at the same rate? What friends have spiritual awakenings at precisely the same moment? What teammates in ministry have come to find Jesus through the same process? We're all on unique journeys, and our individual timetables are unique. Our fear of pain will tempt us to try to adjust their spiritual journeys and shorten their timetables. We could easily start to manipulate instead of facilitate their spirituality.

You've seen it happen. She goes on a retreat; he stays home resentful. She comes back from the retreat excited; he is threatened. She gets involved in the parish youth group; he sits at home watching television. She brings the whole family to the parish picnic; he goes, but he's grumpy all day.

They're on different timetables. But he feels she's taking off without him, and she wishes he'd hurry up and get involved. Actually, both people are hurting and wish the other partner would do something about it. One hurts, waiting for the partner to grow; the other hurts, watching the other person grow without him, always getting excited about something outside their relationship.

I've seen marriages break up over this, producing ministry widows and widowers. Many times it's the man who creates the difficulty by suddenly becoming spiritual. For years the woman was the spiritual person in the family, getting people to church, insisting on grace before meals, seeing to the children's religious education. Then after all her effort and without much help from her husband, he suddenly joins a prayer group, reads the Bible every day, and tries to take over the spiritual leadership of the family. She's threatened, and the two partners find themselves in a turf war over spiritual roles.

So sometimes we fear the pain of waiting for the other person to grow; other times we fear the pain of having the other person grow unexpectedly. Either way, if the two people plan to stay together, there must be honest dialogue, and that will involve more effort. The fear of pain will invite the participants to view this struggle as a waste of time.

And yet, pain is not the enemy; fear is. A doctor once reminded me that pain serves an important function: it's a signal that points to the real problem. If you break your leg, the pain and swelling help you locate the break. If you were to deaden the pain before locating the break, you might try to walk on it and injure yourself even worse.

But many people do just that: they deaden the pain instead of treating the injury that caused the pain. Look at the amount of advertising that offers to help people with their headaches, tension, acne, loneliness, and unpopularity. If the product isn't marketed to reduce physical pain, then it promises to help you relieve relational pain. The physical-pain relievers promise you peace; the relational-pain relievers promise you popularity and friendship, and even romance. They play on our fear of pain. None of the advertisers, however, shows us how to mend a broken heart. But God does.

Could pain be the call of God for us to grow, to struggle to stay in relationships? Could this be a way God has to point out our spiritual injuries? Then, instead of avoiding the pain because we're afraid, we can deal effectively with the real damage, the relational problem causing the pain. It's OK to be a hurting Christian. God is not happy you're hurting, and you certainly aren't happy with the pain either, but it can be an opportunity to grow.

The pain of relationships can happen when parents need to let go of their grip on their children, or children need to leave home: painful moments that we might block out if we are afraid of the pain. It can happen between friends who share the consequences of each other's mistakes. It can also occur as spouses begin allowing space for each other to grow on different timetables. These same spouses might realize that it's better to wait in pain for the long-term growth that will really last instead of a quick, but manipulated, resolution.

Learning to live with pain, and not let it distract you or make you choose the wrong response in relationships, will reveal you as a person who loves the way God does. You'll be joining God in trusting the free will of those you love. You'll hurt from the destructive choices of others, but you won't try to take away their right to choose. You'll watch people you really care about make terrible choices after you've showed them better options.

No one understands the process of waiting for people to grow better than God does. If we are going to wait with the Lord, we will have to come to terms with our fear of pain. Waiting means being vulnerable with the persons we care about. It involves loving them while still respecting their freedom. Actually our willingness to deal effectively with our fear indicates the strength of our commitment to them.

Once we get in touch with this fear and begin to overcome it, we will begin to see something some other people might not wait around to find out: good can come out of a bad situation. God can bring good out of evil. It seems paradoxical, but making mistakes is not necessarily bad. In other words, in avoiding mistakes and living too cautiously, you may never live at all!

The fear of pain can keep us from risking hurt in order to grow. And it can keep us from allowing others to risk being hurt so they can grow. This fear will make us preoccupied with preventing hurt, suppressing hurt, avoiding hurtful situations, even blocking people from taking risks. And we use that lovely sounding excuse that can be so destructive: "But I didn't want them to get hurt." Maybe we are genuinely concerned that people we love not be crushed by a bad experience in a relationship. That's a healthy concern. But many times our concern is only for ourselves: we're actually afraid of hurting *with* them as a result of their choices.

Watch God in the same situation. He helps people review the options, pointing out the destructive choices along with the life-giving ones. But he will not intercept the consequences once an individual chooses. Instead he waits around, offering his power to help us deal with the consequences. He doesn't seem to be afraid of our being hurt, nor does he try to avoid hurting with us when we make the wrong choices.

Actually, it's refreshing to see that God isn't going to blow us up when we choose an option that hurts. He seems confident that at least the consequences of our choices will teach us even if we're not going to listen to his advice and guidance.

Whether we learn from God or from the consequences of own choices, we will have the opportunity to learn how to reverse some of our bad choices by simply making some good choices. And sometimes we can even escape the damage brought on by our mistakes.

But that won't happen very often. So we'll just have to learn how to handle pain. Ultimately, we won't be able to avoid pain any more than we'll be able to avoid occasional failures and rejections. But this pain doesn't have to destroy us. It can be turned into an opportunity before it becomes a problem.

Sadly, the fear of pain might never let you get this far. This fear might have you convinced, if you let it, that you cannot survive the pain. It might make you avoid that pain at any cost. It might have you so distracted by the possibility of being hurt that you won't let yourself grow with someone or stay in your commitments.

And yet, the power and presence of Jesus Christ certifies that you can survive pain, you can survive struggles that loving others requires. You may still hurt at times, but you won't be destroyed. In fact, your painful moments can make you a better minister because you'll be more sensitive to other people's pain. Christians who have suffered while loving deeply become people of hope because they've survived their own pain, and they can testify that pain is survivable.

Jesus isn't just a heavenly pain reliever, even though he certainly offers physical and spiritual cures. When we can't get rid of our pain, he simply joins us in our pain so we don't have to experience it alone.

Of course we won't have to go out looking for pain to prove we can conquer our fear of it. Pain has a way of finding each of us, and no matter how many times we have overcome our fear of it, the next time we confront it, it will still not be easy. But we can be confident that Jesus Christ will be at our service within us. And in Jesus, we have an experienced friend. It wasn't easy for him either.

Fear of Death

No matter what mental tricks we play on ourselves or on others in relationships, and regardless of the many ways we have manipulated others to take responsibility for our actions, death is the equalizer. It is one event we must experience for ourselves.

In a materialistic society, death is tragic. If I am what I do, then death terminates my activity, ending both my meaning and my existence. As a consumer, I can no longer consume. "The consumer is consumed by consumption," one wag put it.

What is it about death that terrifies us? Is it the unknown? Do we fear losing control of our future? Do we fear we will be alone? Or do we fear that we will *not be* at all? That we will cease existing?

It seems that no matter what the church says or what the doctrine of the communion of saints reveals, we still carry a deep fear of annihilation. Nothing in the scriptures, the life of Jesus, or even our prayer experiences can completely erase our profound suspicion that when we die, we're going to pass out of existence. And this fear cannot be resolved completely until we actually experience death. This feeling of fear will be with us until we know for sure that there is more to life than our material eyes can see. And the only way to know for sure is to die.

Must we therefore go through this life controlled by this fear? Or can we address our fear effectively through the many messages we are offered by the only one who really knows what death is: God? Can we see in our experience of Jesus that learning to die is part of living, part of being Christian? Will we spend this life fearing death and denying its results, or can we learn from the Lord incarnate in all creation that we need to die spiritually and physically to be completely happy?

Dying spiritually is part of growing in friendships and partnerships. There are times when what you want, what you prefer, has to be put aside in order to care for someone else. You will have to die to your desires, preferences, even some needs; you will have to sacrifice for another person. When you die to yourself, what happens to the relationship? It grows! It is enriched; it even rises to a new level of life. "Unless a seed dies, it remains only a single grain" (John 12:24).

Nothing shows our willingness to die spiritually more than forgiveness. Forgiving someone means dying to our own hostility and killing our desire for revenge. And asking for forgiveness involves dying to our selfish pride. Whether we seek to be forgiven or agree to forgive, something destructive in us will have to die, usually our self-centeredness. But it can feel as though our identity is being extinguished.

Anyone who has loved deeply knows the kind of dying demanded by forgiveness. "The person who has been forgiven little, loves little" (Luke 7:47). In offering forgiveness to someone who has hurt us, we are really saying, "*You* are more important than your mistake." And in asking forgiveness of someone, we are declaring, "*We* are more important than my mistake."

Every time friends or partners hurt one another, there is an opportunity to grow by forgiving. I can either let my selfishness die, so we can keep living, or I can destroy our relationship, so my grudge can live. Some people are much more in love with their own feelings than they are with their friends or partners, so they will want to keep their feelings alive—even the bad ones—rather than keep the relationship alive. We tend to keep alive what we value the most. "Where your treasure is, there will your heart be also" (Matt. 6:21).

Forgiveness says that I value you more than I value my fears. I won't try to kill your selfishness; that's something only you can do. I can die to mine. But the fear of death might not let me choose this kind of dying if I strongly fear the possibility of being reduced to nothing in this relationship.

So the more we die spiritually, the more we can see new life. Isn't new life the result of dying? How many ways do we have to be told that dying is more than just a scriptural promise? It's a way of life! And if you can discover in your relationships and in nature around you that new life is a result of dying to destructive things, then why not choose to live that way now? And if you have died often and died well, learning in the process that the cycle of death and resurrection is real, then when you die for the last time, you will live forever. Your final death will reveal that you are finished dying, not finished living!

A Christian is not someone who dies once, but someone who dies often, because it is a means to live fully. Death is simply a doorway to more life.

The more you live in this world, the more you become part of all creation, the more you will see the cycle of death and resurrection. The seasons are part of this cycle. Water is part of this cycle. Jesus Christ, incarnate in creation, is part of this cycle. And we are part of this cycle.

We can fear dying and ignore what we see. We can try to avoid entering into the full experience of this cycle. We can creep through this cycle timidly, with our brakes on, resisting all the way. We can let fear distort reality, telling us that death is the end of life.

Or we can let the laws of nature and the track record of our satisfying relationships confirm God's promise that *life is the end of death*. And by dying well, by experiencing what our fears say cannot happen, we expose our fears as liars and show the world that we can live fully even in this life. There is life even beyond fear.

So why do we fear death? That's easy to ask, but you and I know that the next time we encounter a problem in a relationship, we're going to hit the brakes. The next time we're hurt, we're going to wonder, "Will I be destroyed if I give in, if I forgive, or ask for forgiveness?" Then our fear is speaking. Our suspicions are aroused: we might be extinguished, we might be made to think we're nothing. We should fight to defend our right to feel hurt. And we should preserve this feeling even at the cost of the whole relationship. We're not going to let that person run over us like that! We don't easily say, "Forgiveness? No problem!" "Oh, death to my self-centeredness? Wonderful! I love it!"

It will be a struggle. Our fear of death might make us resist every opportunity to die spiritually. But the Lord of nature, the Lord of death and resurrection, Jesus Christ invites us to live beyond this fear so we can live in abundance. And even if we accept this invitation, our fear will not disappear. But we can move away from its dominance over our lives. We might still resist our daily deaths and resurrections, but we will be aware as we look back on our experience of God, friendships, and nature, that death is not the end of life. Life is the end of death.

As we move into new situations and new relationships, we know we have choices. Our past experiences can confirm what the Lord is trying to tell us: we can survive dying, both spiritually and physically.

Part of dealing with the fear of death is learning to allow others to die, even helping them to die well, and trusting that they will survive dying also. Sometimes the way we spend time with them betrays our real attitudes about death. We may claim to be Christian. We may recite our doctrines about life after death. We may join our prayers with the saints in heaven. But we won't allow friends or partners to die well, because we fear obliteration of their existence, or at least the termination of our relationship with them.

But the people we care about need to feel our faith. It's difficult for them to deal with their own fears and ours too. Although it's true that they are the only ones who can do their own dying, they can gain support from our faith. They need to know that we believe in them, in their life, more than we believe in their dying bodies. We have to believe enough in their survival so that they can choose to believe in it themselves. And finally, when they do die, we have to deal effectively with our sense of loss by reminding ourselves that we never owned them. They always belonged to God, and now live "face to face" (1 Cor. 13:12) with him. In death, the veil of flesh is pulled away to reveal the permanence of his power and presence. If death completes the revelation of God to someone we love, why should we fight against it? Fear. And once again, this time through the death of a loved one, God invites us to *forgive him* for taking this person to himself. Once again we are challenged to die to our own selfishness and rejoice that another person has died for the last time and found the permanence of life.

All of this may sound simple, but of course it isn't easy. One area in particular where we hate to see death is within the church. As ministers, we say that the church is the body of Christ. The church is the people of God. But the institutional or organizational part of church may mean a lot more to us than we would care to admit.

To all you youth ministers, religious educators, parents, clergy, and anyone else, whether wearing a title or not: is it permissible for the organizational church to die and rise?

Maybe I'd better ask this question another way. Is it OK for your parish to die? Is it OK for your youth group to die? Is it OK for any organized process to die? And will there be life after that death?

Is there life after parish councils and budget cuts? Can I survive without an official title? Can I build new relationships, even build a new community after moving away from an already well-built and exciting one?

Is it OK for some things to pass into history while we find new expressions of the same power and presence and new forms to celebrate our relationships with God and one another?

True, the church as the body of Christ will always remain alive in some form. God will never change. But we will. And change means that something dies; something else shows up. Some traditions disappear; others take their place.

And Jesus is at the center of this change. It wouldn't be wise to bet that the same Jesus, who changes water to wine, who feeds a hillside of people with a few loaves and fish, who dies and rises himself, and who turns bread and wine into himself, and then calls us to *metanoia* ("change of heart"), won't juggle some of the traditions and images of the church. If Jesus can change the body to reach the heart, he will. "Don't be afraid of the one who can kill the body. Fear the one who can kill the soul" (Luke 12:4).

Over the centuries the organizational models of the church have changed often, always in the attempt to reveal what cannot change: God's love for us, his presence in us, and his power working through us. We do not serve the organization; the organization serves us. "Man was not made for the Sabbath; the Sabbath was made for man" (Mark 2:27).

Instead, we work for and with God. As in any good relationship, sometimes we help him, sometimes he helps us. In changing some of the forms and images, he is only saying that we are more important than the organizational details. We can trust that he will not change what is essential and central to his power and presence. But to keep the essential things in focus, he will see that the organizational church flexes a bit.

I agree that not all change is good, nor is it all from God. So we need to stay alert constantly as to which changes are destructive and which are from God. There are many "wolves in sheep's clothing" (Matt. 7:15). My own experience has taught me that changes that challenge my selfishness are usually from God. Changes that promote my comfort and ease are probably not from God.

Our fear of death will always encourage us to keep alive the forms in the organizational church that sustain our selfishness. This fear will motivate our fight to preserve certain traditions and practices, even after they've outlived their usefulness to the whole church. We may be hanging on to them just because we're comfortable doing them, even *good* at doing them. So if the change in these practices comes along and the Lord finds us clinging to them when it is better to change, he will be asking us, "So, do you worship this tradition or practice more than you worship me?"

Jesus is far more interested in keeping our relationship with him alive. But like any relationship, it will constantly be developing and changing. Jesus is telling us to "fear the one who can kill the soul" (Luke 12:4), in other words, watch out for the fear that will keep your real self from living.

The fear of death can kill us where we mustn't die; it can ruin our confidence and trust in God, making us doubt what his word tells us. This fear can even make us doubt what our eyes, ears, heads, and hearts tell us. If it is allowed to run our lives, it will keep us preoccupied with our own destruction so much that we might even cause the termination of the only thing that can make us completely happy: life with God.

Jesus Christ, with all his power and presence, has placed his whole kingdom at our disposal, trusting that although we have the freedom to live forever in isolation, we won't choose that disastrous option.

Jesus Confronts the Kingdom of Fear

If God had remained in his safe heaven we might be able to accuse him of not understanding how it really is down here. We might hear God's message to "love one another as I have loved you," and respond, "That's easy for you to say! Do you really know what loving costs?"

But God, by virtue of the Incarnation, has decided to experience the human condition with us. Jesus Christ is God come to earth. He is Emmanuel ("God with us"), the word made flesh.

In Jesus Christ, God has become more human than we have even allowed ourselves to become! And he turns to humanity and challenges us to get involved in becoming fully human. Because we cannot abandon our humanity to go to God, God comes to us, enters our humanity, and shows us that being human is perfectly compatible with being divine and with loving the only way God can love: unconditionally. Typical of God, he has taken away our excuses for not being happy. We can no longer claim that God is an uncaring being way up there. We can no longer witness his unconditional love for us and still wonder if we are worth anything. And we can't even accuse him of being a puppeteer, dangling all of us on strings but controlling our choices, because the gift of free will has placed our happiness and fulfillment totally within our grasp, if we choose it.

If we were totally helpless, then God would have to do it all for us. Instead we have plenty of choices, lots of freedom, and the power and presence of Jesus Christ. God is living with us to show us how to live.

We cannot sit back, then, and ask God to do all the work. We aren't helpless! And God won't tolerate us using our humanity as an excuse for not joining him in sharing his power and presence in the world. He has chosen to do his loving through us.

Part of the experience of being human involves dealing effectively with fear. Even Jesus experienced fear, but overcame it. He invites us to do the same and even shows us how it's done. As we learn from him how to deal with fear, we can join him in announcing to the world that there is life after fear. Through Jesus, and with our help, the world can find out that the way to happiness, the truth that satisfies, and the life that cannot be destroyed is a person, not a technique.

Jesus has come to reveal the unconditional love of God, and this is announced within the human condition by a God-Human who experiences our fear. And he shows us that there is success after failure, acceptance after rejection, peace after pain, and life after death. If we don't believe him now, what more can he do, short of taking away our free will and forcing us to be happy?

Jesus Christ did not become human so that we wouldn't have to be human. And he didn't experience fear so that we wouldn't have to. He came to reveal. He came to pull back the veil, the shroud that conceals our goodness. And in a series of events that we celebrate as Holy Week, he shows us clearly how to deal effectively with our fears of failure, rejection, pain, and death. If he had given in to any of these fears, his mission would have ended and his message would have been counterfeit.

Jesus Confronts the Fear of Failure

At the time of the public ministry of Jesus, the Jewish nation was occupied by the Roman empire. This was not just a political problem for the Jewish people; it was a religious problem. Any Jew who studied God's activity in Jewish history knew that whenever God intervened to save them from invasion, exile, isolation, or any other difficulty, he would always rescue them as a whole community, as a people. This always brought about some political changes within their community, and also within the power structures through which they interacted with other cultures. In other words, God involved himself in world affairs, the politics between nations. It was part of the salvation experience. Politics were deeply integrated with religion and the promised Messiah would, of course, have a combined religious and political mission.

Because of the Roman occupation, the people living in the time of Jesus were certainly ready for a Messiah! Jesus claimed to be king of the Jews. Then let's throw the heathens out of the promised land! No one at that time would have asked more of God. But God had more in mind.

Jesus could gather crowds, get them excited, cure them, speak of God from his own personal relationship. He could obviously lead; in fact, he could lead so well that the leadership in the Jewish temple was profoundly threatened. Should they get behind this Jesus and overcome their own pride? He might be able to pull off a coup. Or should they destroy his "attempted revolt" and maintain their accommodation with the Roman governor?

For different reasons both the common people and the religious leaders were interested in the mission of Jesus. But all of the people operated out of an expectation, based on their image of God, that dictated some political expression of any salvation experience brought by a Messiah.

If Jesus had been so task-oriented as to think on the basis of his popular reception upon entering Jerusalem, amid waving palm branches, that his mission was political, then he would have submitted to the motives of the crowd, but not been faithful to his own mission.

Imagine his fear of failing in the eyes of these people, of letting them down in an area where they clearly expected help from God. But whose expectations must he meet? What would be wrong with throwing the Romans out of our God-given territory?

Jesus must have realized that if he stayed faithful to his real mission, this crowd, waving palms today, would soon be waving their fists instead, once they found out that he had failed them.

Jesus afraid? Yes. But yield to that fear? No. Jesus sticks to his own mission in the face of his fear, so that he can renew these people and show them a revelation beyond their expectations. This love he will reveal will change people, and then these changed people can change their own political system if necessary.

With the love Jesus is offering, anyone can be free no matter what the political system might be. With his unconditional love, Jesus knows that we can be free within any political system. We don't have to change systems in order to love and be loved. Some political environments, of course, may be more conducive to loving than others but God isn't going to wait for one system to win out over another before people can find happiness. In order to prove this, Jesus avoided a political overthrow. He clearly placed personal relationships above organizational systems, and he put religious renewal ahead of political renewal.

Isn't this a challenge to all of us who would like to see the church reorganized politically before the individual people within the church are renewed personally? If you can't pray because the liturgy isn't celebrated the way it used to be, then God has news for you. If you can't minister to people who have needs because someone in authority isn't running the organization properly, then God is challenging you. If you can't serve the needs of God's people because there is injustice within the church, then you are saying, "I can't love until there is political renewal."

Instead of blessing political ineptitude and corruption, God is reminding us that politics will never be perfect. We might be able to improve some political situations, but they will never be perfect. We might be able to improve some political situations, but they will never be perfect. Lovers don't have to wait.

Anyone can carry out a mission of love, just by being more loving within the relationships already available.

The Lord's mission is to free people inside. And if happy and loving people want to reorganize society, then fine. But systems and organizations, no matter how well designed, will never love you. Only people within these structures can love you. In confronting his fear of failure, Jesus is saying, "People are more important than systems." And he invites us to follow him.

Jesus Confronts the Fear of Rejection

At some point in his mission, Jesus has to deal with the anxiety of his personal friends and followers. When the tension becomes high, who will stick by him?

We can see that his friends are erratic. Peter is especially mercurial, swearing by him one moment, then denying him the next. When things start to go sour politically, when it is obvious to everyone that the worldly messianic mission is not going to happen, and reprisals are in the works, Jesus doesn't give in to his fear of being rejected by the people closest to him.

He doesn't say to this group of panicstricken followers, "OK, guys. You can come back. I was only kidding! We can slip out of town tonight. Sorry I scared you." Instead he continues his mission, even at the cost of losing his disciples. Not even a rejection by Peter "denying me three times" (Mark 14:30) and the dispersal of the rest of his followers stops Jesus.

His closest friends abandon him as he is arrested. They're bailing out. Smart people aware of the spiritual politics know that good messiahs don't get thrown into jail. It's not good for the mission! And if the mission is going to fail, I'm not going to be a casualty!

Why doesn't Jesus call the whole thing off? Why endure the process of redemption? Why care about people who don't care about him? Why love people unconditionally who stay in relationships only when it's comfortable? God frustrated? Yes. Afraid? Yes. Alone? Yes. Give in? No.

Again Jesus confronts his fear and reveals a commitment to us that is not shaken by our lack of commitment to him. Our choices do not control his choices. But his choices are an invitation to discover the life that awaits us as we overcome, as he did, our fear of rejection.

Jesus Confronts the Fear of Pain

Here again, as with the Jesus' miracles, is a physical event with a spiritual equivalent. No one likes pain. And the physical pain experienced by Jesus was designed by his executioners to be brutal. Scourging and crucifixion were intended to be a deterrent, reminding the general population that this was the punishment they could expect if they didn't behave.

I'm sure the physical pain was incredible. The spiritual side of pain is the key part of Jesus' proclamation that when you love someone, you hurt with them and for them. No one can seriously love without being hurt. If you ever come to the point in a relationship where it isn't worth it to keep hurting, then you'll stop loving.

So pain had to be a part of Jesus' message. Love certainly has its happy moments. But loving someone deeply includes becoming vulnerable enough to allow yourself to be hurt by the person you're loving. If you keep your defenses up and wait until the person you claim to love is so perfect that he or she can't hurt you, you'll never love. If your love is greater than your fear of pain, then prove it!

Jesus reveals that his love is greater than his hurt. He endures his fear of pain because we're worth it.

Is there anyone we know who is worth more to us than our fear of pain? Jesus invites us to declare ourselves in all our relationships and reveal with him that love is greater than our fear of being hurt.

Jesus Confronts the Fear of Death

What do we fear the most about dying? The unknown? The loneliness? The medical problems? Leaving friends? Certainly all of that. But the deepest part of that fear is a nagging suspicion that when we die, there will be nothing. I dread that I will *no longer be*!

This is the fear of annihilation, the fear of becoming nothing. And despite what God tells us, we wonder if these promises aren't just a trick to calm us in the face of death.

So Jesus makes this fear part of his proclamation, and he personally confronts the fear of death in his own experience. You might say, "Fine! He was God. He knew he wouldn't be annihilated. But we're only human."

But the same God who knows he won't be annihilated also knows that we won't be annihilated either! If you were God and knew all of this, how would you try to communicate this to humanity? Become human and die—and then show up again!

Jesus confronts his human fear of death and invites us to confront ours. He dies without deserving the violent and early death forced on him. But there is a reason he dies: to show us how to die and to show us the result of dying, which is more life.

Dying is the only way to get out of this world alive! And relationally, it's the only way out of selfishness, the only way to keep a relationship alive. Physically and spiritually, Jesus shows us *how* to die, and even better, *why* to die.

And then he comes back to life at his Resurrection, saying, "See! There is life on the other side of death. Now that I have done it, I invite you to come, follow me."

Jesus challenges us to see behind our fears, to challenge the illusion that the material side of life is all that exists. He calls us to run at the brick wall of death and discover that it is only a veil that parts and reveals more life behind it.

We don't have to confront this fear of death alone. The same Jesus who has broken the spell of death lives with us now to join us in our struggles and confrontations.

Jesus Christ doesn't die *for* us in the sense that we won't have to die. He dies to show us how to die. He makes dying an act of love and an act of revelation. And the person who can learn how to die to selfishness and fear will find the fullness of life waiting on the other side of the veil. "Even if he dies, he shall live." (John 11:26).

But all of the experience of Jesus, all of his revelation, all of his invitations to us can only clarify what our choices really are. He will respect our free will. "Here are the choices. I've shown you how. And I will stay with you while you choose and deal with the consequences of your choices, but I cannot do it for you."

To do it for us, instead of allowing us to do it ourselves, would be to cancel our free will. How can you love without choosing? And how can you choose without free will? Jesus, knowing what our life-giving choices are, and trusting in us, can only wait for our response. And waiting is something God does well. He's been doing it for a long time!

If we were God, we'd probably do things a little differently. We probably would have canceled this experiment in free will long ago, saying that it was a nice idea, but it cost too much in casualties. We would then have taken control over people's lives and made them happy in one sweeping blast of love. And because everybody would be happy and choices would no longer be a factor, then there would be no struggle, suffering, or war to terrify people. People would have everything they needed—except the power to agree to be happy.

Maybe it's better that we aren't God.

The Resurrected Jesus and His Body: The Church

The events of Holy Week are the proclamation of the power and presence of Jesus Christ conquering everything that can destroy us. In these events, Jesus clearly shows us that he is revelation, not replacement. He is our model, not our substitute. He is our strength, not a confirmation of our weakness.

Jesus did not fail as a political messiah so that we wouldn't have to deal with the same questions. He dealt with his fear of failure in order to show us how to deal with it.

Jesus didn't suffer rejection so we wouldn't have to; he showed us how to deal with the same fear. And he continues even now to show us. We will be rejected at times. He told us that (Matt. 5:11). But we don't have to be overcome by that fear.

Jesus didn't suffer so that we wouldn't have to suffer. He showed us how to suffer and how to make suffering redemptive in our relationships.

And Jesus didn't die so that we wouldn't have to die. Of course we're going to die! So he shows us how to die. Remember, a good Christian dies well, and dies daily. Our final death should celebrate all the dying we have done and become an entry point into the unlimited part of life, which we have already begun experiencing in a limited way here on earth. We don't have to be turned away from dying well. Our fears are real, but they can be overcome.

At last the veil has been "ripped in two" (Mark 15:38), parted to reveal our God no longer hidden behind sin and guilt, no longer disguised as a cloud, or even hiding within a temple built of stone.

In the Christian Tradition God is still hidden, waiting to be discovered. But now he is veiled in flesh: *in carne*. He dwells in the new temple, our bodies. In the New Testament the temple of worship is made of flesh. We are the place where God happens. Our bodies are his body.

We become the place people can go to find God. We are the resurrected body of Christ, the tangible way he presents himself. "He who hears you, hears me" (Luke 10:16).

When Jesus loves, he loves through us. When he touches, he uses our hands. When he smiles or shows concern, he uses our facial expressions. At all times he remains here, working and redeeming through us. People will come to us for glimpses of God if they cannot get in touch with the power and presence of God within themselves.

The "Word made flesh and dwelt among us" (John 1:14). was and still is Jesus Christ. He is seen in the scriptures as "sitting at the right hand of the Father in heaven" (Mark 14:62). Well, the Father may be in heaven, but the right hand is the working hand. And where is the work being done? Here! Up in heaven the work is all finished. Here is where the work continues. And Jesus is doing the work of the Father by revealing the Father's saving love and working through us to display that love.

Like the seventy-two disciples who returned from their ministry expedition amazed that the power really worked (Luke 10:1–20), we are called to help "Satan fall like lightning" (Luke 10:18) by claiming that same power of healing and renewal.

Now we become part of the revelation event, showing people life beyond barriers, love without limits or conditions, and happiness even while suffering and struggling.

The scriptures reveal these events as the story of Jesus continues. After his death and resurrection, Jesus begins appearing to people to show that he really is alive. Most times it was obvious that it was Jesus, as when he appeared to them in a closed room (John 20:19). It didn't take the disciples long to figure out who he was. "It's Jesus!" It was important that his friends still recognize him.

But on three occasions after his resurrection, he looked like anyone else. On the walk to Emmaus (Luke 24:13–33), he joined two discouraged disciples and showed them that the messiah must suffer and die. Later on the journey they recognized him in the breaking of the bread. In the garden Mary thought he was the gardener (John 20:15). On another occasion the disciples were fishing and noticed a stranger on the shore roasting a fish (John 21:6–9). On all three occasions the people who had spent the most time with Jesus failed to recognize him immediately. Maybe that is part of the revelation: sometimes Jesus will be recognizable as the Son of God, the messiah, or in any of his well-known images. But there will be times when Jesus, the Incarnation of the Father's love, will look like *anyone*—you, me, the person next door.

After he spends forty days convincing them he's really alive, he commissions them and then leaves. Or rather disappears. The body he has been using is taken from their sight, appropriately veiled by a cloud! But after promising to remain with us all days, even to the end of the world, Jesus cannot really have left. After declaring that whenever two or three are gathered, there he would be in our midst (Matt. 18:20), certainly Jesus would not be going back to his safe heaven, there to rest peacefully while we struggle.

Jesus may have been "taken from their sight" (Acts 1:9), but he didn't leave us. The Ascension simply removed one body of Jesus so that the new body—the church—could start developing properly. It would be hard for the church to live up to its claim as the body of Christ if the original body of Jesus were still around! And you can't understand or imagine Jesus Christ without his body. We can't separate the second person of the Trinity from his dwelling place and still understand him as Jesus Christ. Jesus is also part of a totally spiritual Trinity, but by virtue of the Incarnation he will always have a body. As part of the three-person community called God Jesus has a face-to-face relationship with the Father and the Holy Spirit, but because he is "at the right hand of the Father" (Col. 3:1), he also does the Father's work in the world: he reveals the Father's unconditional love for us. And when you work in this world you need a body, or at least some visible and tangible form.

So now we see the fullness of the revelation. The Father is intent on loving us and makes that love visible in the flesh through Jesus. Jesus is the revelation of the Father's love. As such, he is called the word of God. A word exists for only one reason: to reveal something. So the Father's love is visible in Jesus Christ, and Jesus needs a way to make that love visible. So he dismisses one body and moves into ours! The Incarnation is the certification that God believes in us. He's moved in! And he trusts that we can join him in making love visible and attractive in the world. In effect, he's trusted the whole of humanity to make love visible. "Anyone who loves has Christ within him" (John 15:9–10).

That could mean that, like the centurion whose faith helped him to be healed even though he wasn't part of the Jewish faith community, any people who genuinely love are expressing Jesus Christ, even though they might not label what they're doing or the love they're sharing. The Vatican II Council agreed that there is some truth in all religions. But I like the comment Jesus made: "Not everyone who says 'Lord, Lord' will enter the kingdom of heaven, but he who does the will of my Father in heaven" (Matt. 7:21). And what is the "will of my Father in heaven"? That all should be saved (John 6:40) from loneliness, isolation, and despair. Anyone who loves is doing the will of the Father and is a part of the body Jesus is proud to call his own.

So Jesus *remains* God and human, using our bodies as his body. Through us Jesus is working to announce his love by loving. And you can't love someone without being in a relationship. So proclaiming the kingdom of Jesus means loving. And loving means relationships. If God is love, then religion is relationships.

Now we are the people in whom God has placed his trust. He believes in us more than we believe in ourselves. He is far more willing to dwell in us than we are willing to dwell in him. Standing within us in the flesh, he issues his offer to the world: Will you accept my love? Will you help me love others? Will you be coredeemers, corevealers with me in loving people in this world and telling them why?

Because of the Incarnation we are the body of Christ, the physical expression of Jesus loving through us, working behind the veil of our humanity to be discovered.

It is not baptism that brings the Incarnation to us. The word made flesh in all of humanity is initiated by God. We can't even choose it. His presence within us is his decision; what we do in response to that presence is our decision. Baptism celebrates our initiation into the visible community of Christians, all those who have formally agreed to be loved by God.

So the Incarnation can be experienced on two different levels of perception:

THE INFORMAL CHURCH

All humanity, who from conception have God living in them. This is the Incarnation from God's initiative. Everyone is born with his presence, accompanied by an invitation to build a two-way relationship.

THE FORMAL CHURCH

All those who have agreed to a relationship with God by silent consent (baptism of desire), by sacrificial commitment (baptism of blood), or by formal sacramental sign (baptism of water).

The formal church is usually a public community that nurtures the relationship with God through word, gesture, and music. This is the way we make the spiritual relationship visible, physical and tangible. As long as we're human, we need relationships that are both spiritual and physical. That's why we have Jesus. He is the best that is spiritual (God) and the best that is human (spirit and body). Jesus is our contact in this life with the Father in heaven. When we accept his invitation to be loved, Jesus leads us to the Father, under the guidance of the Holy Spirit. The only way to the Father is through Jesus (John 14:6). In other words, you can't meet God "out there" until you meet him *here*, within your experience, within your flesh, within your brothers and sisters.

Now that God is within us and between us, the cycle of our involvement is clear. From our very creation, we are good. Living within that goodness is God incarnate in us. This God in the flesh is Jesus Christ. Through the revelation of Christ, we are invited to be loved unconditionally. When we accept this invitation, the Father's love can work its wonders within us. We find ourselves being healed and renewed by this love. And then, because it works so well in us, we are asked to announce this saving love to others. This is ministry. We join Jesus Christ in loving people and telling them why!

PART TWO: THE WEDGE

The Wedge

As Part One has shown, Incarnational theology is based on God's decison to take up residence in us and also to offer a relationship that saves us from loneliness. Our choices are to either accept or reject this offer of a relationship. Fundamentalism sees God taking up residence in us only after *we* make a choice to let God in. So our acceptance of a relationship also includes permission to arrive. In Incarnational theology, however, we see that human nature is veiled, not destroyed, by the Fall, and humanity continues to remain the place where God dwells. And so, although the Old Testament temple is made of brick and stone, the New Testament temple is made of flesh. We are that flesh, and Jesus has made us his residence.

The body of Christ is now the church that "flowed out of the side of Christ" according to Pope Pius XII's encyclical on the "Mystical Body of Christ" (1943). So the church begins at the death of Christ: as one body dies, a new body begins to live. The new body of Christ—the church—is all humanity, informally, and all baptized Christians, formally. The manifestation of the church happens at Pentecost, when the Holy Spirit comes over the church in hiding and sends the apostles out to become the church on a mission, continuing the work of Jesus.

When we go out to do ministry with others, we are visiting a place where God is already at work. Our job as ministers is to join Jesus at work with each individual. When we minister, we are loving people in a variety of ways. But what does real loving actually look and feel like? When we sift through all the theological language, church titles, ministry programs, and especially all our relationships, how do we know we are loving? How can we tell what people really need? How do we join God, who is already at work in another person's life, and how can we make an effective contribution to the growth of that individual?

In this part of the book, you are invited to look at how a diagram that I call the wedge has begun, grown, and changed. For many this wedge has been a helpful window and clarifying tool that hosts numerous ministry issues.

The Original Wedge

Since 1972, when I began a new assignment as youth director for Humboldt County in California, I have been developing the wedge diagram to help people see the various pieces of ministry connected together. The original flow chart diagram wasn't actually a wedge design, but a three-layered cake design I borrowed from Lyman Coleman, author of *Serendipity*, with whom I had worked for six years. I simply took the main issues of youth ministry (reaching, teaching, and keeping youth) and worked them into a cake design that looked like this:

CHART 1: *The Ribbon Cake Wedge*

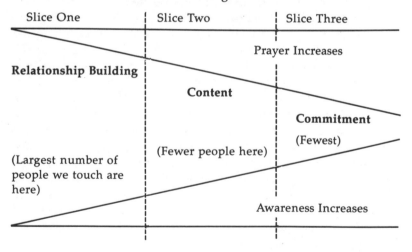

What is this diagram saying? Moving from left to right, we cut slices in our cake (represented by the broken lines) as we saw how various people grew during their personal and spiritual journeys. As the diagram shows, in the first slice we found we were spending more time on relationships, "taking people where they were at," to quote the phrase of the time. As their growth progressed, the composition of each slice changed. In other words, as they grew, they weren't as nervous about their relationships with their parents and peers as they once had been. As their relationship issues diminished, they expanded their horizons to include an increased awareness of God, social justice, outreach, and the church. Each new slice of the cake shows that although we initially spent most of the time talking about what *they* were concerned about, as time progressed, they would develop an interest in the deeper issues *we* were concerned about.

We gradually discovered that most people—including youth—worried most about their relationships. How do we build good, satisfying relationships? And how do we stay in good relationships and heal from bad ones? Because most people worried about these issues, we spent most of our time working with them here. Thus the first part of the wedge is widest because most of the people we dealt with were working on their relationship building.

Some of these people eventually needed to move on and reflect on their relationships in more depth. The wedge notes that their numbers were smaller than the numbers in the first group. They wanted to know how others in society and in the church worked through their relationship issues with God, others, and themselves. In responding, we found ourselves reaching for the techniques of psychology and counseling as well as for other spiritual and doctrinal resources of the church: moral and sacramental theology, scripture, and spiritual direction. In short, we were introducing religious content as our appropriate response to the questions these people were asking. And it worked. It was just what they were looking for: a reflective tool to help them look back upon their own relationships from the perspective of the experiences and conclusions of people throughout salvation history.

Finally, some of these people were so satisfied with this experience of the church helping them build good relationships and understand how to use religious content to grow in their spiritual/relational life that they were ready to commit to this as a way to live their lives. They were having a good experience of church and wanted more. They were choosing to live their lives this way, permanently. They were committed. The wedge shows that this group is the smallest in number, although the third slice also indicates their *expanded* growth in prayer and spiritual awareness. The numbers were down, but the quality was up.

Now we had a diagram that helped us define what we were learning and a tool we could use to teach others how to help people grow spiritually and relationally. Eventually we realized that the words *spiritual* and *relational* could be used interchangeably.

The Wedge as Window

The wedge, of course, is only a way to perceive: a window that can help us see. Over the years, in response to many suggestions and reactions, I have refined and reshaped the original wedge, all the while knowing that people's lives and the issues of ministry are complex, because life is that way. But seeing is the beginning of loving better, and I am hopeful of giving you a clean window, at least!

In time this design developed and changed. It was put to new purposes as new realizations occurred and as more ministry issues were worked into the design. Eventually the middle layer of the cake design became dominant, because prayer with God and awareness of self and others are also relational events. It became clear that our relationship with God and with others was the task of religion, so it was included in the middle section, which, when lifted from the cake design, looked like a wedge. Thus, chart 2 (the "cakeless" wedge) was developed, which shows that as you look out of your experience into other people's lives, *most* people are struggling with their relationships, trying to survive. *Fewer* have moved past the building/ survival level and are trying to understand what's happening and what's supposed to happen. And then there are those—the *fewest*—who have dedicated their lives to living as fully as possible in relationship with God, others, and themselves. Thus the wedge, which is no longer composed of cake slices, represents a continuum of ongoing experiences.

Knowing that our work as ministers is to join God in progress in an individual, we realized that the wedge could be helpful in identifying the progress of a person's growth. At the same time it could also help ministers read that person's needs and offer the proper response. Thus the wedge also helps us narrow the search for answers to basic ministerial questions: How does a person grow? What can I look for in a person to discern my proper response? How can I facilitate this person's growth?

Look back on your own life and you'll see a *series* of significant people. You've been growing—and these significant people have loved you, challenged you, and helped you accelerate your growth, depending on both their talent and perceptiveness and your readiness and openness.

When you discover that it's now your turn to become significantly involved in the lives of others, the wedge can help you identify what each individual needs, what Jesus is already doing in each person's life, and where you can join Jesus at work. As we reconceive the wedge in its ministerial functions, it looks like chart 2.

CHART 2

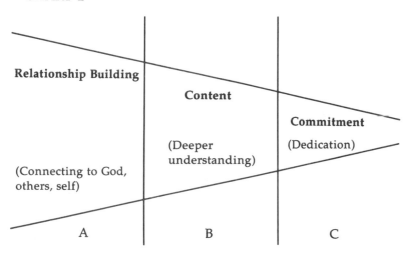

Relationship Building

Content

Commitment

(Deeper understanding)

(Dedication)

(Connecting to God, others, self)

A   B   C

Let's look at each of these three sections, as they pertain to the ministry of the church, in some depth:

Section A: Relationship Building

Because God is already in people, one task of the church is to form and facilitate good relationships that unveil God's presence. Most people you encounter are preoccupied with building and surviving relationships. If you can help them do that, they'll listen to you. If you can't they'll ignore you.

The church cannot continue to proclaim a message of love without showing people *how*. We are, in a sense, competing with the world of business, which markets its products with the promise that people can relate better using these products. Advertising says, "If you want to be happy, buy this product; if you want relationships, buy this product."

The church must get into the marketplace and model the message—not just announce it. Helping people build effective relationships is the task of the church for most of the people who need to hear us.

Section B: Content

As people learn to relate, they need information to help them understand more clearly how to continue relating effectively.

People in this second group have made consistent contact with others in relationships, but they don't know what to do next. The church, however, has the content of a tradition, lasting centuries, that we can bring to bear on the issue. We have the whole salvation story, as well as the local church's story, which should illuminate and enhance the individual's story still in progress. So content connects all three stories: my story, our story (local church), and *the* story (salvation history).

Section C: Commitment

Once people have made contact with others and have drawn upon the experience and knowledge of others in the church currently and historically, then these people will want to dedicate themselves to personal and spiritual growth, and even help others grow as well. This committed group is the smallest number of people you will see through this window, but the most effective and helpful in the church.

Needs We Can Meet

The form of the wedge continued to develop and change as I saw new ministerial uses for the design. During a discussion with a friend, Father Bob Miller of the Diocese of San Bernardino, I was sharing my frustration over the fact that programs in the church aren't always run in order to meet the real needs of the participants. Many times programs are run just because they were run the year before. Participants are forced to attend the program out of their own sense of guilt or by the edict of a parent or some other authority figure. If a program were really meeting the participants' needs, each person would attend freely.

So I was telling Bob we should design programs to meet real needs. He suggested using the Maslow pyramid as a way of identifying what research has done to show us what people need in relationships. Much of the language of the pyramid has been changed over the years, and the needs broken into new segments, but the major needs are still intact. As charts 3A and 3B show, it is possible to examine these progressive needs in light of the concerns of three sections of the wedge. Remember, these are progressive needs, *not* stages of growth, and getting these first five needs met is essential to the relationship-building process.

CHART 3A

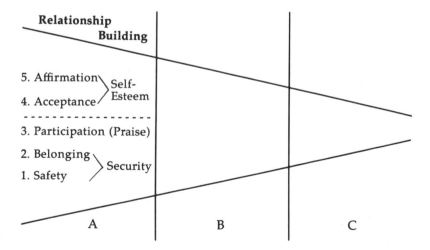

1. Safety

Ultimately, safety is the bottom line in any relationship. If you aren't feeling safe with an individual or a group, you will keep your defenses up and will not grow. If you are not safe, you won't learn, volunteer, relate, and you won't reveal anything of yourself. You certainly won't love—or allow yourself to be loved!

In many of our programs, instead of being concerned about the basic safety of our participants, we first talk about grades (threat), test papers (threat), memorization (threat), and God's laws, all of which can help—*later*. But first we need to be hospitable. People need to know they aren't going to be destroyed by academic or athletic failure or by the judgments of peers.

Whether we do ministry with groups or individuals, our first concern should be for the psychic and spiritual safety of each person. Is this kid scared? Is this adult terrified? First I need to reassure the person before I can reach him or her with any content. Look back on your significant school or program relationships and find your favorite religious person. He or she could be a teacher, a coach, or a parent. What do you remember about that person? Chances are it won't be what he or she taught you. You will fondly remember that the person cared about you, made you feel safe.

Can we create that kind of memory for someone else—today? Safety simply means that I know I'm not going to be wiped out here. It doesn't mean I've chosen to stick around. It doesn't automatically mean I'm going to choose to grow. It simply means I'm in a safe environment physically and relationally.

2. Belonging

Belonging is the need to take a stand somewhere, with some person or group. I already know I'm safe here, but I'm safe other places too. But with this person or with this group, I feel like I want to be *known*. I want to fit in. I want to stay.

You may be safe in ten different places or groups, but you might only belong, or really believe you can reveal yourself, in two or three places.

Belonging can't be caused by a program, no matter how safe

or hospitable it may be. Belonging happens inside the individual and is completely within that person's control. We cannot make someone belong. What we can do is provide a safe environment and a relational invitation. When the individual is ready and chooses to belong, we will see it happen.

Together, safety and belonging merge to produce security.

3. Participation

Once an individual feels safe and has decided to belong, he or she will need to initiate more contact with others in the group. We don't have to get people to participate. Once they are safe and know they belong, they will initiate contact, they will volunteer for projects, they will speak out; in fact, they will *need* to participate. You won't be able to keep them out! I continually hear adults complain about youth who won't participate in liturgy. "How do we get them to participate?" they ask. At the same time, young people often tell us that they don't feel safe in church, or they don't sense a way to belong— to be part of the celebration. They say they're bored. But the real problem involves recognizable music, symbols, and, especially, relationships with other worshipers.

If we could create opportunities in liturgy for them to feel safe and see whether they could belong, then I believe *we could not keep them from participating.* They would *need* to participate once their needs for safety and belonging were met.

The next two needs are crucial to the human development of any person, but for an adolescent they describe the ultimate task: the search for a positive self-image or self-esteem.

People need to be loved unconditionally by at least a few persons during a lifetime. And this unconditional love is expressed in different ways, based on the situation of those being loved. When they do something bad, they need to still be accepted. When they do something good, they need to be praised. And at all times, they need to be affirmed!

4. Acceptance

If people being loved have fouled up somewhere, they need to know that they are still accepted and valued—not because of their behavior (which is unacceptable) but because of their per-

sonal worth, their goodness, their *selves*. And accepting someone who has performed unacceptable behavior is a delicate
task for a loving minister, but it is an absolute *need* for the of-
fending individual. God doesn't like what the person did, but
he doesn't discard that person for the offense. We shouldn't
either.

Acceptance does not mean that I accept your behavior or that
there won't be unpleasant consequences for negative behavior.
It means that your poor behavior can be forgotten. Accepting
someone means saying that *you* are more important than your
negative behavior. I still want a relationship with you. Most
people have never had that message spoken to them sincerely.
This is the purest form of forgiveness. This is unconditional
love of someone who is determined to show me that he or she
isn't lovable. When I love like this, I am loving as God loves.
And although that my be a great spiritual challenge for me as a
minister—it remains a major *need* for the person I'm loving!

Remember, we are distinguishing behavior from the person,
contrary to the American culture, which says you *are* what you
do. In Christianity you are more important than what you do.
Acceptance doesn't have to mean approval of behavior. The
Pharisees were hung up on that issue and were scolded by Jesus for it (Matt. 23:5).

Society says that you can't *be* someone until you *have* something (riches or talents) or *do* something to achieve your worth.
In Christianity your worth is already granted to you. Only the
church carries this responsibility to proclaim people's worth by
the way we love them. And caring for people whose behavior
is unacceptable is one of the clearest proclamations of unconditional love, the revelation of the power and presence of God.
Revelation helps you find it; morality is the way you express it.
Even Jesus reveals his identity as "I am" (John 8:58), not "I do."

5. Affirmation

People also need to know they are worth more than the good
things they do. Affirmation means that I see your worth, your
value, your beauty and I show it to you. When I affirm you, I
am letting you know your good qualities. Too often we water
down affirmation to mean recognition of good behavior. Good

behavior needs to be reinforced, of course. But that's where praise comes in. Praise is for the behavior. You don't affirm someone for putting on a good car wash. You praise him or her for that because it's a good deed. You don't affirm someone for planning a good liturgy. You praise his or her achievement.

Affirmation, on the other hand, is an expression of unconditional love that says, "Although I will praise you for your good actions, I value you as a person even more." It says, "I like your openness. I like your ability to care about people." These are not just good deeds. These are qualities, and are part of the person.

You'll note that I have inserted a dotted line between Participation and Acceptance on chart 3A. This line indicates a division between conditional acceptance (below the line) and unconditional love (above the line); the distinction is important as we try to understand people at different stages of life, especially adolescence. During any period of growth or stage of life, it is useful to understand who influences the individual's values. During childhood, a shrinking time in our technological age, the child comes first to the parents for values and approval. But once that child transfers his or her primary dependence for values and approval from the parents to peers, that child has entered adolescence. Today we can see nine-year-old adolescents.

Before an individual can move from adolescence to true adulthood, he or she must be able to regularly make decisions without being controlled by others, especially peers. Of course, a true adult listens to the opinions of others, but doesn't surrender control to them. By listening objectively to others, but depending on his or her own values, the genuine adult will no doubt gain the approval of others, but not be controlled or dominated by the need for approval, except the approval of God, who teaches us that approval and unconditional love aren't the same thing.

So adolescence is expanding to include nine-year-olds and sixty-year-olds: anyone who allows peers to dictate values and approval. Once you give others the power to dictate your values and approve your actions, you give them the power to control you by their conditional acceptance of you. And conditional acceptance, when it is used by peer groups, will offer you the "security" of safety and belonging and even allow you to "participate" with the gorup. But a peer group will never let you cross the borderline from conditional acceptance to unconditional love. A contract is forged in anxiety and sealed through the codes of behavior. You can belong and we will protect you *if* you follow the behavioral codes of the group.

Through this conditional if, a peer group dictates its values and assigns its approval, controlling the individual with conditional acceptance. For example, the peer group, in effect says

- You can be safe here *if*
- You can belong *if*
- You can participate *if*

The nature of the if can vary, but obedience to it will remain the test of loyalty whether you're a teenager or a so-called adult:

- If you wear what we wear.
- If you drink what we drink.
- If you listen to the music we like.
- If you drive the cars we like.
- If you avoid the people we don't like.
- If you talk the way we talk.
- If you join the right club.
- If you are seen at the right parties.
- If you raise your children "right."

Some sort of condition always binds the peer group together, and it's a trap you've entered because of your need to belong. If you break ranks, you're out of the group. Because the strongest personality in each group controls the group, then that person sets up the conditions for acceptance. Acceptance with no conditions is the only way out of this trap.

Until someone offers you unconditional love and you accept that offer, you can never cross that line and grow. You will only move through life accepting one condition after another and belonging to one group after another, never becoming aware of your value and worth given unconditionally by God. This worth needs to be revealed by someone who loves you unconditionally and won't manipulate you or try to control you for his or her own selfish reasons.

If the opinions of others still control you, you haven't crossed the line. If you have to compete to prove your worth or achieve something in society in order to feel valuable, then you still have not discovered the free gift God is offering. We often allow ourselves to believe we have become independent of other people's control when actually we have only transferred the control from one group to another. Teenagers are a classic example: they break away from the control of their parents, who can no longer tell them what to wear, who they can hang around with, what music they can listen to, or what opinions they can express. They're free? Not really! Their parents may not control them, but their peer group does: it dictates what to wear, who to hang around with, what music to listen to, and what to say. Later, dating or marriage partners may control them with that same destructive power: conditional acceptance.

A peer group that loves you only if you obey their loyalty codes doesn't really love you at all. It is a peer trap: a place that you can never leave. Only someone who can love you unconditionally—showing you both acceptance and affirmation—can help you cross the line to true freedom.

Has the church sometimes been a peer trap? Have we loved only those who have behaved a certain way, withholding acceptance and forgiveness from those who have failed the loyalty code, but who seek to be reconciled?

Is that the way Jesus works? In the Gospels he deals with some people whose behavior is unacceptable according to God's law. But he treats them as relationally acceptable—even lovable. He offers a personal invitation to love. If they choose not to accept, then that's their choice. But if they want to love and be loved, he welcomes them, even as he warns them to avoid the behavior that can interfere with their true worth.

When you have been accepted and affirmed unconditionally, you will eventually find your true worth. When you like your worthwhile self, we call it self-esteem.

If you are in a relationship with a person or a group where these five needs are being met, then you've got a great relationship going! And you're ready to move to the deeper revelation of yourself, of others, and of God that's illustrated in chart 3B. No one will have to talk you into looking for further revelation. You will seek to know more about yourself, others, and God and then look for ways to celebrate what you've found.

CHART 3B

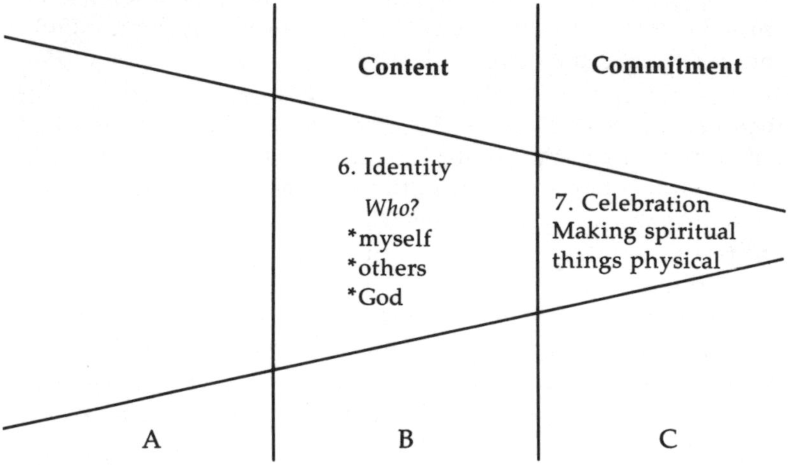

```
                    Content          Commitment


              6. Identity
                 Who?              7. Celebration
                *myself           Making spiritual
                *others           things physical
                *God



         A            B                    C
```

6. Identity

Once you begin to like who you are, then you want to know more. Identity is the answer to the question Who? Of course, one major question involves knowing myself: who am I? But knowing myself, although important, isn't enough. The last thing I want to find out after searching for myself and finding myself is that I am someone, but I am alone!

So I need to know who are the significant people in my life. Who am I with? is a major issue. Who loves me? Whom do I love? Others will be a part of my identity, especially if they have played or are currently playing a vital role in my life. So my family, my friends, my enemies, my teachers, my church, my heroes will influence my self-image, which then affects my worldview.

Finally, God is someone I need to know—not just know about. In God, revealed through Jesus Christ, I find myself, my worth, my meaning, and my happiness. My pursuit for identity must include real answers to real questions: Who am I? Who am I with? Who are the others in my life? Who is God? Which of these individuals do I love? Who loves me?

This is where content aids in the search for identity. The content of Christianity operates at its fullest and purest when it answers the question Who? The other questions—the What? When? Where? Why? How many? and How? questions—are subordinated to this main question. This is consistent with the teaching of Jesus in summarizing the whole law into the two great commandments: Love the Lord your God, and your neighbor as yourself (Mark 12:30–31). In other words, love God, others, and yourself. When that is happening, the kingdom is happening. Revelation is happening. Salvation is happening. Ministry is happening.

Somebody is loving. Someone is being loved. And someone is being revealed more fully. Information (content) is the result of relationships. Information can only supply summaries of successful and unsuccessful relationships. These historical summaries can teach, guide, enlighten, challenge, and proclaim God's call to us, inviting us to be loved. And information can help us reflect on our existing relationships so we can clarify and improve these relationships. But information can go no further than that.

Information is not God. Information is not a relationship. Content will never love you. It is a great servant to relationships when used properly, but it's an unforgiving master when used improperly. When religion begins to worship its own information rather than the Lord the information is supposed to reveal, then our religious educational systems have created a false god, elevating a servant to the stature of master. Jesus is the Lord of hearts, not the Lord of systems.

Many of our pathways, steps, and stages have become, for

some people, dominating systems guaranteed to produce holiness, or at least an accommodation with God. But we don't need to make deals with God to secure his love and providence. It's free! No strings attached. Here we can dismiss superstition as part of true religion because no ritual, rite, or behavioral code can earn God's favor. No bargains need to be struck with God to get him to love us and take care of us. He already does! Free!

In the gospel, Jesus is not revealing a new system, a new code that unlocks the heart of an angry Father in heaven. Our Father in heaven isn't angry. He's just frustrated that we won't accept a free gift!

So Jesus is revealing himself and his offer of unconditional love. He said "I am the Way, the Truth, and the Life" (John 14:6). He did not say "These steps are the Way; this secret behavior pattern is the Truth; this information is the Life."

Jesus is the way to the Father's love. And Jesus is still here *in carne*. So the way is here. Jesus is the revelation of the Father's love, so the truth is here. And Jesus is the fullness of life—so the abundance is here now. The power is in the presence, and the presence is incarnate within us and between us.

Any information that can assist us in bringing the whos together in love—of God, others, and self—is valuable. And so the main task of our religious content is to reveal these identities and to clarify for us the need to discover our goodness, our worth, our unique personalities, our lovability, our world around us, and the significant people in our lives. But none of these discoveries will make much sense without meeting God and growing in a personal relationship with him. We *need* a God who makes us confront our pain, so we can be healed and renewed.

We don't need a God who will be satisfied with our veiled personalities. We don't need a God who gives us spiritual band-aids instead of real cures. And we don't need a God who will do *our* will, allowing us to take the easy way out of problems or protecting us from things we should confront.

Ours is a God of identity, a God of revelation, who loves to proclaim a kingdom of who: God and his people in love. He is the answer and we are the reason. The rest of the questions can only supply supporting information.

Our proclamation should always help to introduce the listener to God. Much of the time we stop short of helping people meet God. It's easier to talk about God than to announce and facilitate an actual relationship with God.

I don't need to be taught about a God with whom I'm out of relationship. I need someone to help me get in touch or back in touch with this God. This is where spiritual direction has such an important impact on people's growth. Information can only supply me with facts. Spiritual direction helps me listen for God, then discern his movement in my life and clarify my response.

Because our God is so relational, the church can best help people by bringing spiritual direction back into the field of education, even children's education. Religious education will never fulfill the meaning of the word *educate* ("to lead towards something or someone") until it becomes a personal spiritual education.

"Now is the acceptable time!" (2 Cor. 6:2). It's time to meet this God we've all been hearing about and to listen to what he has to say to each of us. It's time to discover God's identity, person to person. It's time for the real identity of the church to be revealed. But in revealing the person of Christ, we will soon discover a Christ who is also desperately trying to reveal *us* as well.

God has unveiled his own presence to us as Jesus Christ, and he has no intention of allowing himself to be the *only* one unveiled. He reveals everything he is—even shedding his body to reveal his inner self. This "emptying Himself" (Phil. 2:7) for us is an invitation to us to allow him to help us peel off our own defenses and become as vulnerable as he is. He invites us to take off our insecurity and discover ourselves behind the mask. Moses only had to remove his shoes before the burning bush. Jesus, in being stripped *twice* at the cross, losing both his clothes and then his body, is asking us to remove all veils hiding our true identity.

So the content of religion best serves the listener when it helps us relate with God, with others, and with ourselves. If content can't do that, what good is it? It will either frustrate me or bore me. I hope it's clear that I'm not against information. I am for information that is transferred in the service of relationships.

7. Celebration

When I begin to get in touch with my identity, and when I have good relationships with others, and my connection with God is growing, I also begin to realize, "Hey, this isn't easy, but it's enjoyable!" God's a great one with whom to spend time! So are my friends! And maybe some people in my life aren't much fun to be with, but I can see they need some loving! This is the time when I'm going to need to broadcast what I've found. Nobody keeps good news to themselves. I need to celebrate what's happening in my life. I need to go public with my love! And because I believe that *celebration means making spiritual events physical,* then I will start putting my growth into tangible signs and symbols that I can use to share with others. And I will seek others to share with, and we will learn to read each other's signs so we can understand and share in each other's growth.

So my celebration, whether it be public or private, will mean taking what's inside me, encoding it into some appropriate behavior, and then acting it out: making visible what it invisible. Again, it is bringing a spiritual event into physical expression.

Celebration is a need when spiritual events are in progress, when love and reconciliation are active in a relationship. But when there is no relationship, no spirituality, and no faith, the acts of celebration become substitutes for real faith rather than signs of it. Many times we expose people of no faith or weak faith to our formal signs of celebration (our sacraments) in hopes of generating more faith. Our time might be better spent in some form of simple spiritual direction, helping the individuals identify and clarify the presence and activity of God in their lives.

Of course we know that sacraments can accelerate faith if the believer cooperates. But sacraments cannot do what God himself does not do—namely, cause faith or accelerate faith against the free will of the person involved. When a person of little or no faith willingly performs a sacramental sign, but is unwilling to accept the spiritual and relational events that the sign is supposed to celebrate, then it is an empty sign and a dishonest celebration. "These people honor me with their lips, but their hearts are far from me" (Mark 7:6 quoting Isa. 29:13). As in all sacraments, God is active (*ex opere operato*), but it takes two to complete the relationship. Another person has to participate willingly (*ex opere operantis*). God always shows up for a relationship. But do we?

We see this with people who want their children baptized into the body of Christ, but will not share their faith with the worshiping community or even the children they had baptized. We see it in confirmation (which is often the sacrament of departure, not the seal of commitment) and in reconciliation, whenever the intention is not to return to any closeness with God or with the persons damaged by sin.

An honest celebration cannot take place unless people have something to celebrate. Of course the tangible sacramental sign is always honest on God's part. And there is some validity to the view that we can never go wrong in offering God's love in sacramental signs—even if people don't accept them. But the best way to celebrate sacraments or any other tangible signs in relationships is with willing participants, people who are experiencing and deepening their spiritual growth with God and his people—all of them.

The "something" we celebrate is our relationships, our struggles, our loves, our hurts, our successes, and our failures. We live our lives discovering God and growing, discovering his Love and sharing it, and when we die for the last time, we see fully unveiled the God we knew in this life veiled in the flesh. We must spend our days on earth building and growing in our relationships. If we are to improve the way we celebrate, we must improve the way we relate. If we want a better Sunday liturgy, we must grow—and help others grow—the other six days of the week.

We must spend less time with liturgical gimmicks and more time working with people. I'm not against innovative liturgies, but the best liturgies I have experienced featured believes celebrating faith experiences with other believers, and in the process finding they have created still another faith experience.

Celebration of Feelings

A full experience involves both facts and feelings, so not only are the facts of our experiences to be celebrated and shared, so also are our feelings.

It seems that finally, in the past few decades, we have begun to appreciate the role of feelings in our spiritual growth, our relationships, and our public and private prayer.

Emotional Spectrum A

For a long time in the church, feelings were suspect. They were to be controlled. If you felt good that was considered pleasurable, and we were told that pleasure was earthly and not a valid sign of God's presence. If you felt bad it was seen as a sign of losing your faith and trust in God. So people were taught to keep feelings under control. The goal was to be even-tempered. No highs and no lows. Stay balanced in the middle of the emotional spectrum.

Emotional Spectrum B

Because of recent renewal movements—Charismatics, Cursillo, Marriage Encounters, Search, and so on—we're seeing more joy and we're starting to find the permission to feel good. People are raising their voices in liturgies; music is becoming more upbeat; we're smiling again and hearing the witness and testimony of people who have found happiness in loving God.

Emotional Spectrum C

But although joy is a real part of spiritual growth, especially during our breakthrough experiences, there are still times of struggle and failure that are vital to spiritual growth. What do we do with our feelings of frustration with ourselves and with others? What do we do with our hurt and anger? How do we express our negative feelings to God and to our faith community? How can we feel negative without feeling guilty, or guilty without feeling unloved, or unloved without giving up? In short, what's missing in the church is the way to celebrate our negative feelings and still stay Christians. We need to incorporate our relational struggles and our ministry frustrations—even our disasters—into our celebrations. What we need are more "Downer Celebrations," ways to celebrate appropriately the negative feelings that are legitimately felt by people who are growing in faith. The Psalms, the writings of the saints, even the music of today can help us learn to *feel good about feeling bad*. We need to allow feelings to be feelings, whether they be good or bad, without panicking or judging them. In suspending judgment we allow these feelings to be expressed adequately, so that they either take care of themselves or they become clear enough to indicate exactly what the problem is and how to deal with it.

One of my favorite memories of a Downer Celebration is of an event that occurred while I was a deacon working with one of my seminary classmates at a mission church in our diocese. Both of us were finished with most of our seminary education and were completing our in-service training just prior to ordination to the priesthood.

We knew all the theories about ministry; we just did not have much experience. As you may know, this is the recipe for ministerial chaos! Despite our careful design and planning, we found the task of building and leading this faith community to be overwhelming. We discovered that poverty was not romantic, the utility companies were not religious, and that people—good Catholics—were having problems they weren't supposed to be having. Their problems, of course, created unscheduled difficulties, provoking in each of us feelings unbecoming a deacon as well as language unbecoming a Christian. All of this generated guilt, which in turn made us question our vocation, our baptism, our friendship with Jesus, the existence of God, and the buoyance of ships at sea!

All of this anxiety evaporated, however, with a ceremony we celebrated each night as we crawled into our bunk beds. We lay quietly—I in the top bunk, Doug in the bottom bunk—and reflected on the day. Then one of us would begin the litany (language edited for pious consumption):

"Two of our checks bounced."

The other would chant, "Oh God!"

"My car had a flat tire."

"Oh God!"
"Three members of our youth group are in jail."
"Oh God!"
"Our water pump was stolen."
"Oh God!"
"The borrowed tractor is stuck in the mud."
"Oh God!"
"The bishop's coming next week!"
"Oh God!"

On and on the litany would go, until our ministerial garbage had been articulated and given a proper response. Usually we were howling with laughter by the time we were three items into the litany, and by the end of the celebration we knew the problems would still be facing us the next morning, but we felt a lot better about ourselves and about God. And with a good night's sleep, we were much more effective the next day than if we had worried all night.

Downer Celebrations are the right and rite of every Christian! And the more we can help people celebrate their anxieties and struggles appropriately, the more real our liturgies and other prayer experiences will become.

The Coiled Arrow of Ministry

For me, the ultimate growth experience is not to be a celebrant and behold the presence of God, although this is certainly a great spiritual experience. Even the apostles, who had highly tangible experiences with Jesus, had more to do. Peter, James, and John, for instance, shared a special vision of Jesus during the Transfiguration (Mark 9:2), and Peter told Jesus that he could be happy staying on the mountaintop and even building three tents for the illuminated visitors. But a vision is not enough. We need to share that vision by helping someone else to grow. Jesus marched Peter, James, and John back down the mountain, back into humanity, back into the valleys, where the soil is richer, where the people are searching for their meaning. Just when you start feeling good about your own growth, he asks you to help someone else. Isn't that just like God?

So growth isn't so much a straight line as it's a spiral, the first helping the last (Mark 10:31), and the last becoming first priority for the celebrant. Chart 4 illustrates that movement.

CHART 4

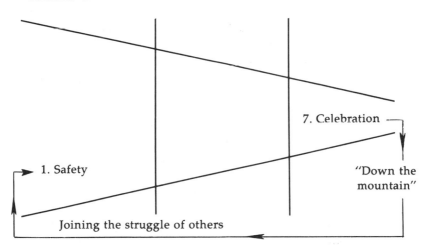

7. Celebration

1. Safety

"Down the mountain"

Joining the struggle of others

Even as we celebrants join the struggle of those who feel unsafe, helping them find some safety with us, we begin to love as God loves. We find that by providing physical and emotional food, shelter, and clothing to the needy, we are offering safety as well. We find some of these people attaching themselves to us and belonging to us. We may even grow attached to them. Of course we still discover our own fears and vulnerability. But in our fears we learn to understand others' fears, and in our vulnerability we love people with less manipulation and more of the unconditional love they need and deserve.

As we join others on their journey, we deepen our own sense of safety, belonging, and participation. We find on this spiral a clearer sense of God's acceptance and affirmation. We see our own identity revealed as God's identity surfaces in the struggles and joys of the people we are helping. And we celebrate these experiences with our positive and negative feelings, and with more and more conviction as we cycle through this spiral over and over again.

If it bothers you that the arrow of ministry is actually shaped like a coil, then don't complain to me. Talk to God. And hope that your spiral-coil is at least moving up, and not down!

To Teach as Jesus Did

In chart 1, we saw the three-layered cake showing that during progressive slices of a person's growth the proportions of his or her various needs and experiences will change. We also saw that relationships are basic growth experiences that can be reflected on and learned from as we choose to move on to more experiences and, we hope, better relationships. As we saw in chart 2, when we build a relationship with another we're meeting one of his or her most deeply felt needs.

In chart 3 we noted that ministry involves meeting at least seven specific needs. And it helps to know which is the primary need in the person's life, so we can join God already at work in this person's life. If the basic needs aren't met, then the more advanced forms of growth cannot happen.

In chart 4 we saw that we never stop growing and that we keep having our own specific needs met even more deeply as we turn into servants helping others grow. If we stop growing as celebrants, we help no one, proclaim nothing, and soon run out of events to celebrate. Then we will be telling only old stories of our growth, but will not have any new experiences that can be shared as new stories.

Now in chart 5 we see that the U.S. Bishops Pastoral Letter "To Teach as Jesus Did" (1972) identified three characteristics of the proclamation style of Jesus: community, message, and service. In working these three vital events into the wedge, we are aligning them respectively with relationship building, content, and commitment. In this chart it should be clear that before we can announce the gospel, we need people who are at least willing to listen, which involves building relationships that generate the trust of the listener.

CHART 5

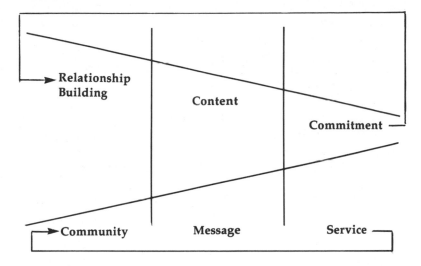

Community

Despite the abundance of such gathering rites as sports, concerts, and political rallies, there is an alarming rise in the rate of dissatisfaction within families, friendships, schools, and working places. Everyone is searching for intimacy, performing the rituals of intimacy, talking "true love" and "forever," but meaning "for now" and "if it feels good." Only God can invite us to forever, and he has. Only the church can claim the commission to announce God's eternal and unconditional love. So the church must also strive to be the gathering of people who embody this message. As a result, the church is always building community, trying to connect people back to one another and to God. Religion comes from the Latin *religere*: "to bind back together"; back into relationships.

Message

If the church isn't revealing itself as the body of Christ, the living organism of loving relationships, then our message is weakened. The world is weary of prophets who claim to know the meaning of life and the power of love. Artists speak of love, as do musicians and psychologists. But so do dog food commercials and cult leaders. The world wants to know who can deliver what is real. And the church needs to move back into the marketplace with the confidence that we are not selling a product that can get people through this life with a minimum of pain. We are revealing that this love is a person who is the way to happiness because he is the destination and travel companion wrapped into one person, who knows the meaning of truth because he is the reality he expresses, and who knows the meaning of life because he is life. And just as Jesus is neither product nor process, but a person who relates to the Father and Holy Spirit as well as to all humanity, the church should never weaken its message to be just a product, process, system, or behavioral code. Our message is Jesus—all of him. And our audience is the people of the world—all of them.

Service

How can you tell when someone loves you? You check to see if he or she delivers on claims. And the clearest way to know how much he or she loves you is to see what it costs to love you—especially when it costs in terms of other priorities such as money, freedom, security, or even life itself.

The Lord presents himself as the suffering servant and invites us to leave everything behind, trusting in his providence, and then to serve the needs of others. We are invited by God to be the visible sign of Christ in the world: his body. And we are invited by the world to be what we preach: lovers who leave behind lesser values to serve the greater—God and his people. Until we serve others, the world won't believe our message. Until we let go of worldly power and use Christ's power made tangible in service, then we probably don't believe our own message either.

Before we can use Christ's power, we have to find it. And we have to find him. If Jesus Christ is incarnate within all humanity and—most important to us—within us and the people around us, how do we recognize him? How do we distinguish his identity from that of the persons in whom he has taken up residence? In other words, God may be in you, but he isn't you. So how do I distinguish him from you?

Moment of Recognition

We have said that the main event in a person's life is meeting God, not just knowing about a God he or she has never met. Actually, at some point during the growth and unveiling of an individual, the activity of God—already working in the person's life—becomes more tangible. This must not be understood as the point in growth where God starts to work in the person's life. We need to see this as the time when God's presence and power are consciously experienced. We'll call this the moment of recognition. No human activity can cause God's power and presence to be given, because this is already a free act of God in the Incarnation. But the church can play a major role in focusing people's attention to look for his presence, and to behold his power wherever it is visible, in the scriptures, in history, in other people's lives, in nature, and especially in an individual's own life.

So when I am with someone else, how can I tell it's Jesus? Simple. When I am loved more than this other person has ever loved me, or when I am asked to give more than this other person has ever asked. And when I am alone, how can I tell it's Jesus? Also simple. I find myself receiving more than I think I need and giving more than I think I have. And I can be alone without being lonely.

CHART 6

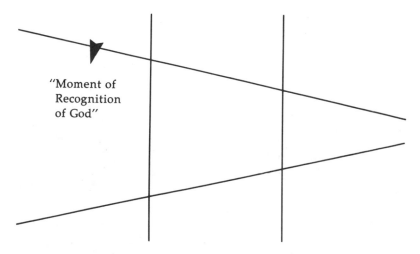

"Moment of
Recognition
of God"

Evangelization, Catechesis, and Vocation

Because the relationship with God is the main focus, our revelation and educational experiences need to keep in mind at all times the recognition of God's activity. When the church is announcing the good news to people who have not recognized his presence and power, then we call this proclamation evangelization. Catechesis, on the other hand, occurs when the church addresses people who have already recognized his presence and power and who need to have this activity interpreted.

CHART 7

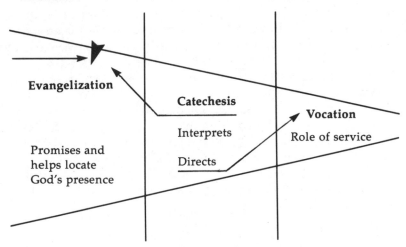

Evangelization

Catechesis

Vocation

Interprets

Role of service

Promises and
helps locate
God's presence

Directs

The main difference between evangelization and catechesis is the person's level of recognition. An individual in need of evangelization clearly needs someone to help him or her to see the good news of God's love is possible in his or her life.

On the other hand, an individual in need of catechesis already consciously experiences this activity of the Lord, but needs the church's help in interpreting this activity. So catechesis, from the Greek word *echo*, is the church's response to the individual. It tracks the activity of God in the person's life and teaches its meaning, not just for that individual; this interpretation also helps the individual see how that activity has been revealed in the local faith community and throughout salvation history. So catechesis combines the process of education with the process of spiritual direction.

There are also some similarities between evangelization and catechesis. Both involve preaching and feature some form of teaching. Both can use the scriptures—especially the Gospel. Both explain salvation history and reveal Jesus Christ and his church.

But the experience of the listener calls us to adjust our preaching and teaching to fit his or her need. We preach and teach differently to someone who cannot identify God's activity than we do to someone who is in touch with this activity.

Unfortunately, some people in the church have used the term *evangelization* to mean "preaching" and the term *catechesis* to mean "teaching," regardless of the state of readiness of the listener. So whether or not anyone in the audience could identify any significant faith experience, if someone was announcing or reading the gospel, it was understood that he or she was evangelizing. On the other hand, a leaders who taught the people in the group about practicing their religion, would be "doing catechesis." In fact, in many circles, the term *catechetics* still means "the tactics of teaching."

Other people are more vague about these two terms, in many cases using them interchangeably. In truth, however, both evangelization and catechesis can include both preaching and teaching. The difference is the faith level of the listener, not the tactics of the presenter. So the announcers and teachers of the good news need to be aware of the faith experience of their audience, letting their preaching and teaching evangelize when there is little or no faith and catechize when there is a developing faith. We need to put preaching and teaching at the service of the needs of our people. When we misread those needs, we try the wrong tactics on the wrong people. We try to catechize nonbelievers and evangelize believers, giving neither what they need.

God's presence is predictable, but his activity is unpredictable, so why is the moment of recognition marked so solidly in one place on the wedge? How can we be sure God's activity will be recognized at that exact spot?

Actually there is no exact spot, because God is God and moves when and where he is ready. So although his movement can and will occur anytime and anywhere, this movement can be promised by evangelizaton and interpreted by catechesis. So I chose to locate this mark of tangible and recognizable activity between evangelization and catechesis.

As always, the readiness of the individual is a major factor in the recognition of God's presence and power. The more aware and open the individual, the more recognition is possible. As a person's basic needs are met, this person grows in awareness as well as in openness. So in meeting other people's basic needs, we are not only performing an act of charity, we are acting out the gospel mandates to feed those who are hungry (spiritually and physically) and to visit those who are sick or imprisoned (again, spiritually and physically). And we are proclaiming the gospel by our actions, helping people move away from the terror of isolation into the experience of good relationships. The less a person has to worry about satisfying basic needs, the more energy that individual can spend experiencing and recognizing God's power and presence. Evangelization is not just announcing with our mouths that God is here; it needs to do what Jesus did in the gospel and continued to do through us today, namely, to *reveal*: to point to God's presence and power. And this is done through the spoken and acted word.

Here again, Jesus, through the church, through me, loves me and tells me why. As I am loved, I am revealed. So are the people who love me and so is God within them and within me. My defenses are peeled away and I let go of them. Why do I need defenses if I'm loved, if I have someone to help meet my needs?

At a certain point during my unveiling, as I feel safe enough to be unwrapped from my defensive package, and as I find a few people with whom I feel I belong, then I start participating in more relationships.

My participation exposes more of me, including my weaknesses and faults, to other people. But if someone can accept me at that point, with genuine unconditional love, and will also affirm my goodness as well, then I will be ready and open to notice God's activity—and to identify that activity as Jesus Christ.

So the mark of the moment of recognition is placed on the

wedge not to tell God when or where to make his move. It's placed where it is to show us that our ministry to people can only prepare them for this experience before it happens or help them understand it once it begins. Once again, remember that we are not preparing people for the beginning of God's activity, because God has been present all through their lives by virtue of the Incarnation. But we can prepare them to make contact with Jesus' presence.

Evangelization by word and deed helps people see this presence. Catechesis by word and deed helps people grow in understanding of the Lord and his power.

Once I hear about a relationship I can have with God and then actually begin having regular encounters wtih God, I will want to learn more about him, about myself, and about other people in my life. My unveiling will continue, exposing my identity. As my identity becomes clarified, God will let me know where in this world my gifts will be needed—where he wants me to minister. This will be a specific call to care for people in a certain way at a certain place. The Lord who has told me he loves me now asks me to pass it on, but not just to anyone I bump into; he asks me to go public with my love, my gifts, and my talents, and to acknowledge his presence and power to others. This call is what we term *vocation*.

Often people limit this to mean a call to religious life or the priesthood. And for a long time it was implied or stated that if you wanted to serve God, you needed to leave everything behind and become a priest, nun, or brother. Today it is clearer that parents serve God too. So do lay teachers, youth ministers, liturgy directors, and countless other people who have heard a call and accepted a vocation to public ministry in the church. All are public servants in the church, responding to God's vocation. But before we give good news, we must first accept it: the unconditional love of God, revealed in Jesus Christ. And this love will be an experience we will always want to share.

Experience, Reflection, and Decision

Whatever is happening to us is our current experience. Everyone is struggling with one experience after another. Before we think, we are already experiencing life. We are sensing, perceiving, imagining, rating, feeling, and making contact with reality around us. So everything we are, and are part of, begins with experience. This is where we meet our friends, ourselves, and God. The world is in love with experiences!

Then, as we accumulate experiences, we begin to reflect on these events, drawing out the common threads as well as the unique differences, forming conclusions, principles, and codes for interpreting other people's behavior as well as developing options for generating some new activity of our own. When we reflect properly, we learn more from our experiences. Fewer people do enough reflection on their experiences.

Finally, our options give us several ways to choose, and using our free will we select the option that we hope will produce the desired consequences. At this point we have made a decision. The consequence now becomes a new experience that should be reflected on, presenting more options. And then another decision can be made. The fewest number of people are making effective decisions, but those of us who are live our lives as fully as is possible. The cycle continues throughout our lifetime.

CHART 8

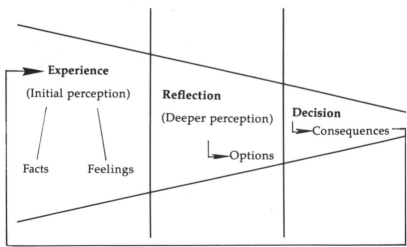

Experience

Ultimately our experience is composed of objective events (facts) colored by our subjective reactions to them (feelings). The facts and feelings that make up our experiences are filtered through our worldview, sometimes even adjusting our perceptions positively or negatively. This filtering process sometimes can distort the experience. If my image of myself won't let me admit that an experience is happening to me, then I will start looking for ways to disguise the experience or disconnect from it altogether. When someone does this, we say that they are living in a fantasy world or perhaps blind to reality.

On the other hand, if I allow myself to behold all that I am experiencing—both facts and feelings—then I am in a great place to make contact with God. Through the Incarnation God enters my experience and can only be discovered and heard and loved within that experience. My humanity is where I meet God. So as long as my experience is clear and accurate, making contact with God, others, and myself is fairly simple. But if my experience is distorted by inaccurate images, then all my relationships will suffer, including my relationship with God.

One of the first things God does within our experience— after, of course, loving us—is to help us discover better images of ourselves so we can perceive the world more accurately and God more fully.

Reflection

Perception during an experience is one thing. Perception afterward is another. Reflection is the human capability to think back upon our experience in order to expand our initial perception of it. With reflection we get a second chance to sort out the facts and feelings after the heat of the moment has passed.

Most of us get more out of an experience after it's over than we do during the experience. As we clarify the facts and listen once again to our feelings, we can develop some objectivity, and read the experience with more accuracy. How many times have we had a disagreement with a friend, then upon reflection, realized that our friend was really right, but we had been too busy defending our point of view to listen properly? Reflection not only enhances the original experience, it also helps us sift out ways to have even better experiences. As a result of reflective scrutiny, we can produce a list of options for new experiences and even review possible consequences for each of the options. So reflection not only helps us look back upon our experience, it also helps us look ahead to new ones, preparing the way for decisions that will set up new events in our lives.

On the practical level, damage can be done when we don't reflect properly. Two difficulties in particular are worth noting.

First of all, because we have many significant experiences daily, both positive and negative, most of us do not take enough reflecting time to process all the facts and feelings, so we end up storing these experiences like cordwood within our psyche. As a result, these important moments in our lives are never properly assimilated, and they stack up, subconsciously pressuring us for our attention and adding to our daily stress levels. Even worse, a major significant experience, when not properly reflected on, will find alternate ways within our personality to gain attention, resulting in neurosis or psychosis. Reflection, then, is not only helpful in reading our experiences accurately and making good decisions, it also is a means to greater spiritual, psychological, and even physical health.

Second, there has been a pattern problem within our religious education process. In the attempt to prepare the student for the future, religious educators have spent more time transferring to the student information and rules for future behavior, and less time looking back into the student's experiences and using the information to help interpret those experiences. Reflection needs to look backward as well as forward. Information is fine, as long as it connects back into the student's experience. Whenever our religious education process misses this important step, the student concludes, "If religion can't help me now, how will it help me later?"

Decision

Reviewing options and consequences can be fun until the moment comes to make the final choice and live with the consequences. Most choices produce several consequences—some good, some bad.

At this point some people hesitate or become indecisive. Others acknowledge the good (or at least, the desired) consequences and ignore the accompanying undesirable ones, assuming they don't exist or that someone else can take care of that stuff.

Decision making, with the accompanying skill of dealing with all the consequences, is the most critical issue in the area of moral development. Whether we are addressing children, youth, young adults, or adults, the issues of drugs, alcohol, suicide, self-image, peer groups, careers, dating, and sexuality are only areas of struggle. The central issue is decision making. People become confused in these other areas when they don't make good decisions, or worse, when they allow others to make their decisions for them. Instead of telling people what to choose, we should quit trying to outdominate the other dominators, and start teaching people how to make decisions and how to live with the consequences, which, of course, become new experiences. And the life cycle continues.

The Combined Wedge

CHART 9

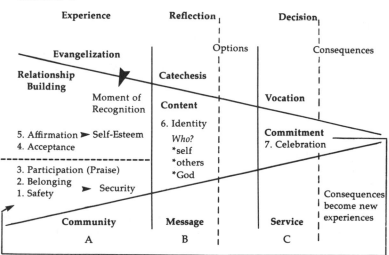

Column A

Our central stance in this world is experiential. Our lives are an experience of reality inside us and around us. Our relationships are experiences and our needs must be met within these experiences. And if, as Fr. Bernard Häring said long ago, "all theology can be experienced somewhere in a relationship," then theology is ultimately meant to be experienced. So we will spend our lives building, surviving, rebuilding, enhancing, and learning from our relationships. We will love and be loved by God, others, and even ourselves in these relationships. In these same relationships we will encounter fear and tragedy, and we will wonder if all of this struggle is worth the effort.

Instead of removing us from stress and struggle, God joins us with his power and presence. And so our theology of relationships becomes an adventure of discoveries and choices. We find our deepest relational needs met by God through ourselves and the people around us. We are bonded to a sometimes loosely defined community, where we find safety and belonging, becoming more secure in the process. In this community of friendships we can initiate more contact with others, thus revealing more of ourselves. In our most vital relationships we are accepted and affirmed, and we begin to sense our real beauty, valuing ourselves as worthwhile people.

As our concerns about meeting basic needs are peeled away by healthy relationships, we stand an excellent chance of recognizing the presence of God in our lives. We may or may not remember that other people, in evangelizing us, promised this would happen, but we will remember for the rest of our lives the excitement of the moment of recognition.

The timing of this moment is not at all predictable, but then neither is falling in love. All we can do is keep relating until these special moments arrive, and, to our amazement, keep happening to us.

Column B

While we are having these relational experiences, we need to keep reflecting on them to discover their meaning and direction. We will be happy to find that we can make full use of the resources of the church as well as the rest of society to sort out and sift through our experiences, identifying a deeper sense of ourselves, others, and God. This is why Jesus challenges us to use his message to seek and find. We can also tap the combined experience of millions of believers and lovers over the centuries, using the content of our faith heritage to clarify and understand our current faith experiences. This is what catechesis does: it helps us interpret our faith experiences and clarify the involvement of God in our lives. Now we know our options.

Column C

As we reflect on our experiences, using the resources available to us, and then comb through our options, we are ready to decide on our next move. We must put our faith into action by serving others who need what we have. We must go public with our love and friendship with God and others, so in celebrating worship with them, we will make spiritual things physical once again through signs and actions. Our whole lives will become a celebration of service, moving our worship beyond the ceremonial and out into the rest of our relationships. We will make these choices because we have committed ourselves to live our faith visibly within our churches and within our world. We are answering a call from God to take what we have heard within the intimacy of our friendship and make it visible as a light to the nations, so that others can share what we have found.

These choices, like all choices, have consequences, which become new experiences, allowing us to join others on their journeys. Our vocations from God will show us where to stand and which journeys to join. Our own personal growth, as well as our service to others, will continue to happen within the arena of daily relationships, until the day when our final vocation calls us face to face with God, who will ask, "Whom did you love? Who loved you?" May our answers take an eternity!

PART THREE:
THE INCARNATION—
A THEOLOGY WE CAN LIVE

The Incarnation—A Theology We Can Live

The beauty of the Incarnation is that we can meet God within the strength and limits of our humanity. A humanist looks at humanity, but sees only humanity, even at times mistaking it for God. The Incarnational Christian can enjoy all that is human by meeting and partnering with God here, joining with God in the flesh, Jesus Christ, in celebrating what is good and in calling to fullness and completion whatever is still incomplete. Certainly evil exists, but it exists within good people who may not have discovered and accepted their own natural goodness yet, and who may not have met and accepted the offer God has made in person from within them.

Because we can't physically leave earth to go to heaven to build a relationship with God, heaven has come to earth. God, in the person of Jesus Christ, has come here.

As part of this whole saga of relationships, free will is the gift that allows us to *choose* whether we will accept a relationship with God and also accept the unconditional love that Jesus brings, which satisfies our human and spiritual hunger and saves us from loneliness in this life as well as the next.

Once we've discovered and accepted God's unconditional love for us and allowed it to begin fulfilling our own lives, then God only asks us to use our free will continuously to place ourselves—as God does—in service to others, revealing the opportunity already awaiting within them. Ministry is simply revealing the kingdom at hand: loving people and telling them why.

What a beautiful use of free will as envisioned by God! And yet, because free will is genuinely free, people can make choices that are destructive to themselves and others. It's easy to look around and see the damage done when people exercise their free will to choose options that do not produce growth or give life.

· Most of us, if we could be God, would cancel everyone's free will, writing it off as an experiment that failed. When you get rid of free will, you get rid of immorality on all levels: personal, social, and global. God's love, along with proper behavior, could then be imposed. God could dictate our happiness, overwhelm our fears, correct the wrongs in our lives, and ensure a happy ending to this story called Creation.

And yet God will not do what most of us would love to do: cancel free will. Instead God keeps trusting us, working with us, hurting with us, celebrating with us, knowing that our faith in him won't be complete until we realize how much faith he has in us. With the Incarnation, we are invited to believe in God. With free will, we are invited to realize that God believes in us.

If free will scares us, then God helps us with our fears. If being loved unconditionally means we must clean up our poor self-images, then a patient God waits upon our choices. If caring for others means we must change our use of material goods, then God shows us our real worth so we can reevaluate our worldly goods, coming to see them as simply tools for the kingdom, instead of a security blanket for a terrified ego.

If we really could cancel free will, we would be eliminating all of this in order to create a problem-free—and option-free—society. Of course we hate pain and human destruction. So does God! But God will not force choices. Our God of the Incarnation is a God of presence, waiting patiently to be discovered. Our God of free will is a God of power, inviting us to choose to join him in loving the world and in empowering people to be happy by their own agreement.

People who haven't discovered Jesus Christ or joined him in a relationship need people like us to be with them, present for them as they search, loving them unconditionally when they fail. This is the way we make Jesus visible and tangible. But this takes time and energy. And often we're tired and impatient.

So what if the world isn't perfect yet? Why abandon hope and wish we could cancel the experiment? Why try to overrule other people's choices? Because *we* don't think we can take it. *We* don't think we can be patient. *We* don't want to struggle with other people's choices and the consequences of those choices.

Thank God we're not God. He would be happier—and we would be happier—if we were a little more human, entering into our humanity as fully as he does. In the process we would grow ourselves and find that we can love people the way God does: by presence and invitation; by trust and forgiveness; and by relationships and power.

If we love people the way God does, then we lead people to God, to happiness, to the kingdom at hand. But like the proverbial horse led to water, we can't make them drink. We can't force their choices.

The power and presence of God is a call to build good relationships with the people around us. This in turn is a call to patience and perception on our part.

Patience: Dealing with Secret Expectations

If we are to show the patience of God in our relationships, we must come to grips with one thing that cripples our willingness to allow other people to make their own choices: secret expectations. Unannounced or even unconscious, these hidden agendas drive us to impatience when we don't see our plan working on schedule. We keep secret *what* others need to do and *when* they should do it, but then we explode when they don't deliver.

As Christian leaders, we can't afford to distort what we experience, or force experiences onto others. Genuine Christian leadership calls forth qualities from people by challenging them to use their love and talents to overcome obstacles. The best leaders are people who perceive situations accurately and understand their people clearly. Communities and societies led by good leaders will live and love more effectively, and reveal the kingdom more clearly. Every one of us is in a position to lead, whether our opportunity happens in the parish, school, street, group, family, or simply in one-to-one relationships.

But although many of us like to lead, when we can't achieve something by exercising our leadership skills we tend to blame those who won't follow us. We might blame the pastor or parents or youth or our spouse or the parish secretary or even the parish housekeeper! Because we can't successfully motivate others, we turn our anger either outward on them or inward upon ourselves. Beneath this anger lies another, more significant feeling. It could be fear, hurt, jealousy, rejection, loneliness, or frustration. If we look honestly into our own experience and identify the major feeling generating our anger, we will also find that this feeling is rooted in an expectation.

Let's say I'm hurt because someone didn't notice or praise one of my projects. Beneath my hurt lies the expectation that this person should react properly. My imge of this person expects this approval. A good reality check might reveal that the other person wasn't even aware of my expectation, and so was in no position to act out what now can only be called my fantasy.

Do you have any secret expectations about the church? About marriage? About ministry? When highly motivated people agree to lead in the church or in relationships, hidden agendas can drive us all to the breaking point. Some people burn out trying to reorganize an earthbound church into being more like heaven. Marriages collapse when one person discovers that the other doesn't share the same vision of the relationship.

Can we love the church even though it isn't heaven? Can we care for people in our lives who don't share the same vision? Can we love people who don't love back? To do this, we must be honest about our expectations; that means being honest with ourselves as well as with others.

Our ability to be patient with ourselves and others will grow in proportion to our level of honesty about our deepest expectations. We may even find that we are becoming more patient with God!

Perception: Staying in Touch with the Incarnate God

If God has entered the secular world and is here working and loving, shouldn't we be trying to find out what he's doing—

and join him? If Jesus has taken on the world's form, but not the world's values, can't we do the same?

Most Christian leaders can function easily within a Christian society, such as parish or family, but they panic when they deal with a secular society in which people aren't living their lives as professed Christians, doing the things Christians should do, and talking the way Christians should talk.

Does Jesus talk only "Christian talk"? Or will he communicate with everyone in a way each can understand? Even though Jesus does not love sin, he does love sinners, and he enters their world, eating (Mark 2:16), drinking, walking, and talking with them in their language.

Can we do the same? Or do we have such little confidence in Jesus' power that we fear being contaminated by the culture of the people who need to be reached?

Even when we learn to pray all day, every day (1 Thess. 5:17), we will discover that the Jesus we are talking with will be manifesting himself both in secular forms and in Christian symbols. At Sunday worship and at other liturgies and Bible studies, Jesus will clearly work through privileged traditional Christian signs, because that's the language we speak and recognize. But don't be fooled into thinking that is the only language he speaks. Jesus, incarnate in our humanity, speaks to all people in all languages and cultures. Just because a culture has flaws it doesn't keep him from entering it and taking on its form in order to communicate himself.

Can we do the same? If we do, we will find ourselves at times praying in a new way: worldly prayer. We will be praying with God, who wears worldly forms while choosing not to submit to worldly values. As Christians, we may have made a mistake in confusing worldly forms with worldly values. Jesus wears the first while rejecting the second.

If we can meet God in the flesh, God in the world, God in the secular form, we will meet Jesus Christ. If we communicate with him in the world, we will see him entering into people's forms of understanding and communication, and trying to reveal his power and presence.

In joining Jesus at work in the world, we will be praying while we are counseling someone, taking a walk, waiting for a bus, or sitting in a meeting. Worldly prayer is dialogue with God in the world, learning from Jesus himself how the rest of the world communicates and believes.

None of this means ceasing to do our work or to communicate within the formal structures of the church. It just means that to be fully announcers of the good news and lovers in a modern world, it helps to be multilingual and multicultural.

Worldly prayer is the companion to liturgical prayer. In both the secular and the "officially sacred" forms, we continue to see new ways of discovering God, and announcing what we have found. Worldly prayer joins liturgical prayer as a partner as we grow in the many ways we can live our Incarnational theology. In this way we join Jesus *in carne,* in the flesh, in the world.

Some people will always see the forms of the world as evil, mistaking these forms as values. But while we squabble over sacred and secular forms, Jesus Christ continues to enter both, reveal in both, love in both, and forgive in both.

Every day I try to be as much a part of both as I can, because I have met Jesus Christ in both; for me, there is no division.

The power and presence of Jesus Christ is here among us. So now my study hall is the whole world; my chapel is any place I find Jesus; and my class each day is the theology of relationships.

A CHRISTIAN'S BILL OF RIGHTS

In the light of the Gospel you have a right

1. To be loved unconditionally
2. To love as best you can
3. To be introduced—personally—to God
4. To know that any experience of unconditional love is an experience of God
5. To know the full name of unconditional love: Jesus Christ
6. To know the whole story of salvation history (*The* story)
7. To belong to a faith community (*Our* story)
8. To share your discoveries and experiences with others (*My* story)
9. To accept God's offer of an ongoing relationship (Faith)
10. To learn how to conduct a dialogue within that relationship (Prayer)
11. To know the many possible moral options available before choosing
12. To ask questions about faith and life
13. To choose, as the proper use of free will
14. To be forgiven at any time
15. To be told why you were baptized
16. To be happy in this life and in the next
17. To live forever

—Fr. Don Kimball

Presented at the Youth Leadership Conference in Dublin, Ireland, in August 1985. Sponsored by the Irish Christian Brothers, commemorating the International Year of Youth.